CHOSEN FATHERS

LIFE LESSONS
LEARNED FROM
FATHERS OF CHILDREN
WITH DISABILITIES

by
ELIYA STROMBERG, PhD

BABAYE PRESS

CHOSEN
FATHERS

Life Lessons Learned from Fathers
of Children with Disabilities

Eliya Stromberg

Copyeditor: Esther Chana Stromberg

Cover Design: Lesley Worrell and Rachaely Eytan

Interior Design: Feige Savitsky

Published in Israel by Babaye Press.

ISBN 978-965-92541-0-1

Version 1.1 (Jerusalem)
Printed by CreateSpace, a DBA of On-Demand Publishing, LLC.

Dedication

My father, Larry Stromberg, and my mother, Helen Landson Stromberg, and my Stromberg and Landson grandparents would have been very proud of me publishing a book that honors fathers. From both sides I grew up with a strong connection to "family," and "father" was a distinct and important role in it. My mother always encouraged me to write because she thought that my letters to home made good reading. I dedicate *Chosen Fathers* to their memory and thank them all for a lifetime of encouragement and love.

Table of Contents

Acknowledgments

It is with thanks to G-d that I have produced this book. It is because of His many blessings and His connecting me to the following people that this book is in print.

It was probably on the first day of class in the program that would lead me to a Master of Science degree in Special Education that my professor, Dr. Ann Dell Duncan, told us that as budding "masters" we stood on the shoulders of giants. Whatever we would learn we will have learned from others, who themselves learned from their giants.

I include among my giants: Dr. Duncan, Elizabeth Haughton, and Eric Haughton (of blessed memory). The massive shoulders of these three people supported me while I learned skills and concepts which directly shaped my professional outlook and career. Their encouragement eventually led me to earn a PhD under the guidance of the giant who taught them, Dr. Ogden Lindsley.

Besides deepening my understanding of how humans behave and preparing me for leadership roles as a school administrator, I credit Dr. Lindsley for shaping my writing style. Dr. Lindsley insisted that each sentence of my dissertation have a subject and an active verb, and be no more than ten words long. He imposed the ten-word rule because, he claimed, "The youth of the day couldn't keep in mind more than one simple thought at a time." In *Chosen Fathers* my sentences have subjects and predicates, but without Dr. Lindsley's orange cross-out pen, the "ten-word" rule was hard to keep.

Rabbi Noach Orlowek travels the world educating educators and parents how to build their children and how to build themselves. For the last twenty-five years I have been learning from him. With thanks to G-d and to Rabbi Orlowek, my three children have turned out very well. I keep working on myself. Himself a published writer and skilled editor, Rabbi Orlowek's advice has significantly shaped *Chosen*

Fathers. In particular, I thank him for suggesting that I detail in the Afterword "life lessons" applicable to all fathers which can be learned from the interviewees. May Rabbi Orlowek continue with strength and clarity to share his wisdom and concern with all of us.

Rabbi Nosson Geisler coached me to announce publicly my long-held secret wish to write a book. He asked a group of aspiring coaches I was part of how many thought I would actually write a book, and almost everyone said I would. So I had to start writing it. That writing project did not become *Chosen Fathers*, but I credit Rabbi Geisler's sensitive and expert coaching with leading me to identify myself as a "writer."

The start of *Chosen Fathers* emerged from a conversation with Rabbi Issamar Ginzberg, a renowned marketing expert. When I asked Rabbi Ginzberg for an effective way to reach people he immediately responded: write a book. He then suggested the interview format. Rabbi Ginzberg made authoring and publishing a book sound so simple that I started to write. *Chosen Fathers* is the result.

I have been able to take the recorded words of the interviewees and create a book because of the expert transcribing by Yaakov Branfman and the skillful text editing of Varda Branfman. Being published writers themselves they understand how much encouragement writers need. I thank them for the verbal "boosts" they each gave me.

Since I am the last person to have proofread *Chosen Fathers* I take full responsibility for any errors in the print that may still exist. But without the very well-trained eye of my professional proofreader, reading the text would have been a major challenge. My proofreader has requested anonymity, but if asked I recommend her without hesitation.

With so many books to choose from today, it is essential to be able to tell a book by its cover. I give especial praise to Rachaely Eytan and Lesley Worrell for their designs of the poignant and engaging cover of *Chosen Fathers*.

Of course, credit must be given to the many fathers who opened themselves up to me and my recorder. Without their willingness to share honestly their thoughts and feelings there could be no book. May they each continue to have success turning life's many challenges into opportunities for personal growth and joy.

Without my wife reminding me that my book didn't have to be perfect, but it did have to get published, I would never have completed this project. Esther Chana is the final editor for all my writing, and her technical and motivational skills are exceptional. Through her I continually discover my writer's voice. But besides giving me her technical expertise she reminds me that G-d has given me talents, ideas, and energy to use to help others. She always has the "biggest" picture in mind, the picture which hints to why I have been chosen for the life I live.

In raising our children, Esther Chana has led the way. Her wisdom and intuition and selfless care are a gift to our special son, our other two children, their spouses, our grandchildren, and to me.

May G-d continue to bless Esther Chana with good health and long life and the desire to work together with me to become the couple we are meant to be.

PREFACE

Every writer has a personal agenda for writing his book.

Here is mine:

- To undo the general impression that fathers of children with disabilities are aloof and uninvolved in raising their child.

- To challenge the agencies which serve families of children with disabilities to rethink their approach to reaching fathers. While most all are successful at reaching out to mothers, few successfully connect to fathers. I know that fathers will accept help if it is presented to them in ways they can use it. The agencies just have to learn how.

- To tell fathers, in a very deep and personal way, that I know raising a child with disabilities is a challenge no father wants. I also want to tell them it can be one of the most effective ways for a father to realize his full potential as a man. And it can be a boundless source of joy.

After reading *Chosen Fathers*, please let me know what you think.

eliya@fathersconnect.com

INTRODUCTION

Life for me was excellent. I was married to a woman whom I continually discovered was truly my "life partner." I was the proud father of a one-and-a-half-year-old boy who was both brilliant and handsome. I had recently moved to Jerusalem, Israel, which I believed was the ideal place to raise my family and myself according to the beliefs and values I held dear. The gift of an inheritance relieved me of immediate financial concerns. My future was filled with hope and opportunity.

And then my second son was born and the future became dark. The doctor said: "Your son has Down syndrome."

In my son's first three months the professionals with whom I interacted never once said: "Congratulations, you have a son! What a gift to be a father! What a source of joy you have been given!" Instead they told me about my son's anomalies, limitations, and disabilities. I was directed to medical personnel who projected scenarios of future development based on studies, norms, and batteries of tests conducted on my son. I met therapists who prescribed an array of regimens to correct my son's "deficiencies." And I received solace and counsel from social workers who would "help me deal with my situation." The message I took away from all this input: my son's existence is a "situation," and for him to have any chance of "making it in the world" he needs professionals more than he needs a father.

I am embarrassed to admit it, but in those first three months I bought in to the message I got from the professionals. I did not feel any joy in being a new father. And I didn't try to bond with my son. The pride I dreamt I'd have from the great accomplishments my son would make as he grew into manhood vanished when I first heard the words "Down syndrome/disabilities." Our newborn wasn't a cuddly source of pride and pleasure; he was a puny, funny-looking challenge to my self-image as a competent father. My son had my genes. Was I somehow "defective"?

Further, it seemed that nothing I had learned from raising my firstborn son would be relevant to this second one. What joy, I thought, could possibly come from a child who I imagined would be a lifelong burden emotionally, socially, and financially? The future spiraled in a "down" syndrome.

Friends were encouraging, but none of them could give me firsthand insights as to what to do about my fears, doubts, and many questions. One friend, however, suggested that I take my son to Professor Reuven Feuerstein, of blessed memory, a world-class educator of individuals with disabilities, to hear from him what he thought about my son. So I did.

When I walked into the Professor's office at the Feuerstein Institute in Jerusalem, cradling my three-month-old son in my arms, I extended my hand in greeting. Instead of taking my hand Professor Feuerstein took my son. After looking deeply into my son's eyes and poking his finger into several places on his scrawny body, Professor Feuerstein looked up at me and said: "You got a good one!" These were the very first positive, encouraging words any professional had said to me about my son. And for the first time I felt (cautiously) optimistic about the future—if I had "a good one" then maybe I could look forward to "good things" coming from him.

The Professor then said to me: "I have a grandson with Down syndrome. Do you know how he came to me? Before his birth his pure soul was flying all over heaven saying, 'Where am I going to go? Where am I going to land?' When that soul looked down and saw me, it said: 'Feuerstein! That's where I am going.'"

The Professor's message was simple, yet profound: I was chosen to be my son's father. And since I was chosen it follows that I must be capable of raising my special son. In fact, since he came to me and not to anyone else, it follows that no other father is better equipped to raise him than I. For the first time in three months I felt good about being my son's father. And immediately my doubts and fears began to fade.

Regardless of one's religious belief, the truth, of course, is that every father (and mother) is chosen. Your child was born to you and not to someone else. However you understand how your child came to you, you must make choices of how to relate to your particular situation. When a child is born and develops in a typical manner a father rarely thinks about his situation. He has before him pretty much what he expected. He may be a "first-time" father but he has plenty of models to follow. He moves forward with a degree of confidence that he will be a successful father. But because we "special fathers" never expected what we got and seldom know (at first, anyway) how to proceed, we become perplexed, stymied, overwhelmed, and often, negative about our situation. We have enough to deal with maintaining normal every day events in our careers, our health, our families, and our marriages. We don't need (or want) "special" problems.

"Typical" fathers manage their families and themselves following "typical" patterns. We "special" fathers have few, if any, guidelines to direct us. Our situation is as unique as our child. While awaiting our newborn or while raising our child who is suddenly traumatized and disabled we never read a book that prepares us for a child with disabilities. But if we are open to it, we can enter into a dynamic life-long process of discovering that we have strengths, sensitivities, and abilities which we never knew of, or expected to have.

There are some fathers who take their unique experiences and become public heroes, like Jul whose interview you will read, championing causes on behalf of their child. At the other extreme are fathers who retreat, unable to ever get beyond their disappointment and their pain. Between the heroes and the retreaters is where most fathers stand. We draw upon our faith in a higher power. We seek support from our wives, family, and community. We educate ourselves. We accept what is and move toward making it as workable as we can. *Chosen Fathers* details how thirteen fathers acknowledged their negativity, accepted what is, and primed themselves for personal growth. For some, it happened with joy.

I interviewed many more fathers than are included in *Chosen Fathers*. Every father I interviewed was genuinely eager to share his personal experience. (Their eagerness challenges the widespread belief that men are reluctant to share intimate details about themselves; men just need an appropriate outlet for doing so; talking to me, a father who shares their experience, was just that outlet.) When some fathers heard the thoughts and feelings which they expressed to me, they discovered that they were not ready to have anyone else hear them. Some fathers shared thoughts and feelings which they had not even shared with their wives. (So many fathers are holding in their deepest feelings; they want relief from their feelings but do not feel safe enough to reveal them.) Consequently, several fathers declined to have their interview published. Nine fathers chose to "go public" but only anonymously. An anonymous interview uses only first names, all of which are fictitious. In the remaining four interviews, fathers agreed to have actual first and last names published.

The children described in *Chosen Fathers* have disabilities resulting from genetic disorders, pregnancy complications, trauma from drug/vaccine reactions, injury, and emotional stress. For one child it has never been determined what the cause of his disabilities is. I made no attempt to present a cross-section of disabilities. The number of labels used to describe disabilities is staggering, in the hundreds. And within a single label no two children's needs are ever identical, so every father's reactions to his child are unique and offer valuable life lessons.

In *Chosen Fathers*, the word "typical" describes children who have a normal birth experience and who do not exhibit any signs of disability.

In common usage the term disabilities applies to physical or mental disabilities. One of the thirteen fathers describes his children's disability as emotional and behavioral, but the children are typical both physically and mentally. How he resolutely faced his children, his wife, and himself earned him a place in *Chosen Fathers*. In truth, just as every parent is "chosen," every child will be "disabled" if he doesn't feel enabled by both his father and mother.

Before my encounter with Professor Feuerstein I was in pain. My dreams and hopes were replaced by doubts and fears. I felt inadequate. I didn't have a clue how to proceed. Not a good place for a man to be.

When I understood what the Professor meant by being chosen, my world turned around. I saw that I had a choice before me: continue to be overwhelmed by the negativity and uncertainty I was feeling, or consider that there is something positive waiting for me to discover about being the father to my special child. I made the choice to start the journey of discovery. And so did the fathers I have interviewed for *Chosen Fathers*.

It is my sincere hope that all fathers will appreciate that they, too, were chosen. And that having been chosen, they utilize all the capabilities they have to build their children and, in turn, themselves. (They may not have all the knowledge they need, but they can acquire it.) I hope further that fathers will learn lessons for living successfully with the challenges they face. That they take pride in seeing their child progress, no matter how slow or how little. And they feel the joy that awaits a man who is blessed to be a father.

Eliya Stromberg, PhD
Jerusalem, 2016

1

MICHAEL

The pregnancy of Michael's wife, Sara, became a threat to her life. They were expecting their first child. Sara's doctors recommended to abort, but the young couple chose not to. Their son, Daniel, was born in the 31st week. It was nearly a year later before Michael and Sara brought their baby home from the hospital.

Eliya: Tell me about Daniel's birth.

Michael: Daniel was born after a very difficult pregnancy. There was not enough amniotic fluid and more than one doctor at the hospital recommended ending the pregnancy. They couldn't see anything definitive, but they thought the chances of Daniel making it were very poor. And they were very concerned about Sara. But we didn't want to abort, so we left the hospital and waited to see how things developed. But as the pregnancy progressed and we saw how Sara was reacting to it, we decided to end the pregnancy. We sought advice from our Rabbi and we were told that given the doctors' concern for Sara's well-being, we could have the abortion.

The hospital's policy was that if you're admitted to the hospital and they see how things are developing and they recommend to abort, they will do so. But once you check out you can't check in again for the express purpose of having an abortion. So once we left the hospital we had no place to go.

I totally freaked out. We had a Rabbinic ruling to permit the abortion, but no hospital to do it in. I called up the head of the department in the hospital where Sara had been admitted and said, "What do I do?" He recommended a well-known gynecologist at another hospital in the city. We called the gynecologist's office and his nurse said, "You can have an appointment in six weeks," and I said, "We have a question of an abortion here. This is critical." So she said, "Come in today at 6:30."

That day, waiting to see the doctor, was the hardest it's ever been. We sat there not knowing if we wanted to kill this embryo, our first child, or if we should keep it alive; whether either outcome would turn out good or not. We hadn't a clue what the doctor would say. That was the worst day emotionally. I've never been through anything that hard since then with Daniel. It was just Sara and me with no family around or friends for support.

Eliya: What happened with the specialist?

Michael: He was amazing. He was a chain-smoker and an unusual fellow, but we felt that we'd come to the right person. We told him the story and I could just hear his brain putting everything together. We felt that he was taking care of us.

We went to ask him whether we should terminate the pregnancy and we ended up continuing it for two more months, because the amniotic fluid had returned. The fetus had stopped growing for a period and then it started growing again. We did ultrasounds, checked this, and checked that. The doctor said, "We'll keep monitoring you and see what's doing." He prescribed medication for Sara to keep her blood pressure down, because it was a bit on the high side. But she wouldn't take it. Sara was very anti-medication and into natural healing.

So after meeting the doctor, we had a reprieve of two months or so, until things got so bad that they had to take Daniel out.

Eliya: What happened?

Michael: What happened was that Sara developed toxemia. Toxemia is a very dangerous condition where the baby is basically poisoning the mother. The only thing they could do was to take out the baby.

Sara's blood pressure went through the ceiling. We went for a checkup and the doctor put Sara right into the delivery room. "Too dangerous," the doctor said. She stayed overnight and in the morning they said, "We think he should come out."

Eliya: How did you react?

Michael: What do you say? Who do you ask, who do you talk to about that? We didn't talk to anyone—we just decided we would take him out. We said, "Okay, we'll roll with the punches. We'll take him out and see what we get."

Eliya: You were all alone in the decision. At the birth did you get any support?

Michael: There was a nurse in the delivery room. She said to us, "You know, these kind of babies, they're fighters." I was encouraged when she said that. But it was very hard at the birth. Daniel was born two and a half months early and weighed only 605 grams.

Eliya: 605 grams? That's less than 1½ pounds.

Michael: Right. Daniel was in the hospital for ten and a half months. For one solid year, my wife expressed milk with a pump. He didn't drink anything for the first three months. He was our first kid, and he was a challenge on many levels.

Eliya: Did you have support or encouragement from anybody after the birth?

Michael: Yes. My wife is a healer, so many of her healing friends were around us. There was one healer lady around at the time who told us the baby was fine. She told us that his name was Daniel. We had not named him yet. Also, we were very close with a very religious Jewish family with ten children. It was two or three days after Daniel was born that I got around to telling them. After hearing the news, the wife was at the hospital within an hour. One other family we were close with also came to visit.

Eliya: What complications arose with the birth?

Michael: In utero an ultrasound could not show for sure what gender Daniel was. At birth it was seen that he had a hypospadias, a malformation of the male genitals. The doctors didn't know if he was a boy or a girl, but the healer had told us that he's a boy, so we knew. Because of the malformation, instead of the traditional way of circumcising the baby on the eighth day after his birth, we had to wait three years to perform the ceremony on Daniel.

Eliya: Three years? Michael, how did you handle all of this? Daniel was your first child.

Michael: I think I'm graced with a positive outlook. Nobody gave us a doomsday scenario or said, "Listen, he's going to be this, he's going to be that." Since they didn't say that he's not going to be okay, I said, "Okay, he was early, but he'll be okay."

I was essentially positive. My motto was: "We'll just keep going, doing what we have to do."

Eliya: After the birth, how did Daniel progress?

Michael: He was in the hospital for a few weeks and he got very, very sick. He almost died at one point. Somebody gave us a book about preemies and I read the chapter about what to do when babies die. But then he got better.

The beginning was hard because Daniel didn't really react to the world. He was eight months old before I saw him look at something. One day the nurse walked across the room and I saw him following her with his eyes, for the first time. I said, "Wow! He's landed!" Until then he was out there someplace.

Eliya: How did you keep connecting with Daniel when you got no response from him?

Michael: It was really difficult. Sara was much more giving than I was. She would hold him, even though there was never any reaction. He was just doing his thing. He was there physically, but not emotionally, as far as I could see.

We didn't have to do much with him when he was in the hospital. Sara expressed milk and we'd come and visit. Every so often she would arrange to hold him next to her skin, with all his tubes and wires. We called it "bonding."

We would see him, but there was no one to react with. So you do what you have to do, but there wasn't a lot to do. We took several videos and we sent them abroad to our families.

I would hold him, too, but there wasn't much to play with. That was a drag. I would think: *He's not here.* I didn't know where he was. We hoped he would be okay.

Eliya: And after ten and a half months in the hospital, you finally took Daniel home.

Michael: Yes, it was very exciting. From an association which loans medical apparatus for free we got oxygen and other equipment. Then shortly after Daniel came home, he didn't need oxygen anymore, which was a great relief.

As we left the hospital, one of the wonderful doctors there told us, thank G-d, that we should expect several hospitalizations every winter.

Eliya: What made you say "thank G-d" after hearing that your son would probably be hospitalized several times per year?

Michael: If he hadn't mentioned that, then we would have had a rough couple of first years. Since we knew what to expect, we were prepared. The problem is that when a baby is that small, they are actually capable of surviving and functioning fairly well—except for their lungs, which are not sufficiently developed to breathe. So the respiratory system is challenged for the first few years, until the lungs grow and develop. In the first years, any virus that came around, Daniel got it. And any cold he caught landed him in the hospital.

Daniel has always gradually gotten better. In the beginning, he was sick every year, and they said to us, "Listen, he'll be in the hospital a lot, but this is one of the few diseases that gets better as he gets older, not worse." As the lungs grow, they get healthier. He still gets sick where he can cough all night, but it's not like before.

Eliya: What was it like to have your son hospitalized just to fight a cold?

Michael: Sometimes it was horrible to watch him. He would just cough and cough and cough, and they couldn't do anything for him. They would just give him oxygen and antibiotics and hope for the best. But when he came out of it he was smiling again.

Eliya: This is the first mention you have made, Michael, of any emotional reaction in Daniel. How did you react to Daniel's first smile?

Michael: Daniel was a little over a year old when he first smiled. I said, "Wow! Now he's a kid!"

Eliya: That smile must have meant so much to you!?

Michael: It did. I remember it to this day.

Eliya: What other special attention did Daniel require?

Michael: In the beginning, he needed lots of medication. He was tiny and needed tons of physiotherapy. I was very gung-ho in those days. I made arrangements with the health fund clinic, which paid for a private physiotherapist to come to the house a few times a week. We had to teach Daniel how to roll over, how to sit, and how to stand. It took him months and months and months until he could roll over. I would practice all these exercises with him. I was very, very supportive. I became this real doer.

Eliya: It seems you were connecting very closely to Daniel.

Michael: I was. It encouraged me a lot that Daniel was responsive, very cute, and very sweet. Plus, I learned an enormous amount from being a partner in his physiotherapy. The therapists would say, "You've got to take him to the park. You've got to put him on the slide." To this day, Daniel has gravitational insecurity. He's not secure in the world physically or emotionally. We all have levels of mistrust, but Daniel's level of mistrust is greater than average. From Daniel's level of mistrust I learned what basic trust means.

Eliya: Please tell me more of what you learned about "basic trust"?

Michael: "Basic trust" is a minimal, "functional" level of belief that the world is okay and that one can survive and flourish in it. Daniel has less of that trust than most people. He is very insecure. He's always worried that a calamity is about to happen, or that he will become sick.

Working with Daniel taught me that basic trust is very relative. I basically trust that things are okay, that G-d is watching, and that I can relax. Daniel doesn't relax that much. His body is tense, and so is his mind. Things that wouldn't upset me at all are difficult for him. Something as simple as choosing to walk home a different way than usual might cause him anxiety. But watching him, I realized that my own level of trust, or of faith, is nothing more than "normal," no great achievement. A wholly righteous person may have a level of trust that's way up high. My level of trust may be lower than that, but it's in the "normal" range, so I'm lulled into thinking that "I'm OK." In truth, I need to work on my trust in the universe, my trust in G-d, as much as I think Daniel does. Daniel may worry more than most of us, but we all worry, and our job is to realize that we don't have to worry. You know that wise saying: "Don't worry, be happy."

Eliya: That sounds like a very deep insight that you learned from your son. Did Daniel ever trust himself on the slide?

Michael: I worked with him for many, many years. I would take him to the park and I'd put him on the slide. He didn't want to go on the slide. "Slowly, slowly," I would tell him. "It's fun, it's fun! Slides are fun!" But they weren't fun for him. Then he would do it once, and I would say, "Wow! You did it!" And then he wouldn't do it again for another four months. It was very frustrating. What happened was that as Daniel got older, I got sort of worn out.

Eliya: What wore you out?

Michael: For long periods of time I couldn't see that my work with Daniel resulted in much progress. I began to think that my son might not be able to progress any further than where he was. I would talk to Sara about it. But she couldn't deal with hearing that it was hard for me. My wife has this Pollyanna side to her. She's always saying: "It's fine, it's wonderful, it's great." I needed my wife to listen to me when I said, "It's hard for me to see Daniel where he's at." But what I got was: "Yes, but… but…but…" I didn't want the "Yes, but…" I just wanted her to hear that it's hard for me. That was the thing we had to work through. Sara had to learn to listen and accept how I felt.

Eliya: Did it take time for Sara to hear you and accept your feelings?

Michael: I don't remember how long, but yes, it was a sore point for a while. Eventually, we went to a therapist, who told Sara, "You just have to listen to what your husband is saying." It took time, but eventually she learned that she could hear me and accept my feelings without feeling the same way, and without feeling threatened. In the end this challenge turned into a big opportunity for Sara and me to learn how to communicate effectively with one another.

Eliya: I am impressed, Michael, how you have been able to take challenges Daniel has presented to you and turn them into opportunities of significant personal growth. Let me ask you, what was school like for Daniel?

Michael: We had a wonderful preschool for Daniel in our neighborhood. The school integrated typical children and children with disabilities. The director was amazing. She put in hours and hours with Daniel. She took videos of him and showed them to a big expert in America and asked him, "What can we do?"

The director would invite me to school after hours to play with Daniel. We were trying to encourage him to interact with me. At that point, though, he was more interested to play "kindergarten" by putting dolls on chairs which he arranged in the room. But he didn't interact with me. I would watch Daniel for a while at his play and then I'd fall asleep.

For several years, I felt deeply disappointed with Daniel and began to think: This is what I get for all of that tremendous effort that I put in—therapy and exercise and taking him all those places?

Eliya: How long did your disappointment last?

Michael: Until Daniel was eleven, which is when he started to eat like a growing boy should eat. Up to age eleven he hardly ate. We took him to several specialists.

He just wasn't interested in food. Once at an appointment with a doctor, Daniel was nibbling on a rice cake. The doctor said, "That's what you give him—rice cakes!? He needs food!" and I recall thinking, "*You* try to feed him!!"

At one point, doctors suggested putting in a gastric tube that would feed him directly into his stomach. But we didn't want to do that. For eleven years, food was just not Daniel's thing, but we made ourselves crazy trying to feed him. And then came the big event. He started eating! His hormones kicked in early and since then he's been eating like a teenager. Today he doesn't stop eating. He's into food, but he's skinny as a rail because he burns it up. Even though he's been eating well for a number of years, seeing Daniel eat still makes me very happy.

Eliya: Did the change in Daniel's appetite change your relationship with him?

Michael: I remember the moment when our relationship really changed. It was on a public holiday and we had been to three barbecues that day. I'd never eaten so much meat in my life. At the last barbecue, Daniel was kind of sailing around in the kitchen and he eyed a tray of brownies and said, "Are these made with milk?" He really wanted some brownies. But there was no way he would touch one if it was made with milk because of the restriction in Jewish dietary laws which prohibits eating milk and meat together. He wanted to know so he could do the right thing. In that instant, I merited to see something that was so beautiful—his desire to do it right, that he was willing to pass on the brownies if they were not permissible. I looked at him and said, "Daniel, you're great!" He looked up at me and it just broke my heart. He said, "Really?" He'd been waiting maybe five years to hear me say that. From that moment on, everything between us changed. It was from that moment on, that moment with the brownies, that Daniel and I became great friends.

I was finally privileged to see who Daniel really is. My wife was always saying, "He's wonderful, he's wonderful." And I was saying (halfheartedly), "Yeah, he's wonderful, he's wonderful." She'd say, "Everybody loves him, he's so cute." And I'd say, "Yeah, everybody loves him, he's so cute." She'd say, "Look, he did that." And I'd say, "Yeah, but what's he gonna be, what's he gonna do?"

Eliya: Prior to that turning point, Michael, what kept you from seeing Daniel as your wife and others did?

Michael: It happened, I think, because of my tremendous effort in doing, doing,

doing, doing. And after a while, I began to think, *This is what you get?* That prevented me from seeing. I got worn out. And then my wife was always telling me how wonderful Daniel was, but I couldn't believe it.

That was the block and, thank G-d, this event happened and it changed everything. Since then, Daniel's great. He's a sweetheart, although he's a pain sometimes when he doesn't get what he wants.

I once met the father of a child with Down syndrome who was also blind and had various other disabilities. It was very difficult for the child to speak. The father called his child "my biggest teacher." The man said to me: "Instead of wanting my child to learn *my* language so he can speak to me, why don't I learn *his* language? He has another way of talking. Who says that my way is the right way, and not his?"

I can't move into that mode myself, but I was very impressed that somebody could look at his disabled child as his biggest teacher.

Eliya: You said, Michael, that sometimes Daniel is a "pain." (And what child isn't?) How do you react to Daniel then?

Michael: When I get upset with Daniel, it's because I think that he's not the norm. But so what? Why does he have to be the norm? He is who he is. I have X amount of patience for a "normal" kid, and he needs more patience. That's what he needs. And I have to be real about that and not have my preconceived ideas about what's normal. "Normal" is only what I'm prepared to do. I wasn't always prepared to do what Daniel needed.

Eliya: What does Daniel need?

Michael: He needs support! And patience. In learning, he needs constant support. Sometimes he says, "I can't do this, I'm stupid, I don't understand it..." I say: "You can do it." I have to be supportive, but it's not easy for me to be one hundred percent supportive. For example, when he's doing homework and he's freaked out, I need to remain calm in the face of his losing it and say, "Yes, you can and it's okay."

It's not easy to be encouraging if I sometimes don't feel encouraged. But I know that is what Daniel needs of me. I need to let go of my ideas of "what he should be" in order to be able to simply see what he is and what he needs. "What should be" just gets in the way.

Eliya: You are a gifted musician, Michael. Have you been able to teach music to Daniel?

Michael: He started to play the piano. That was great, but it was also very awkward because he couldn't take any direction from me. Or maybe I couldn't give it to him in the way he could accept it. It was very uncomfortable and awkward. Several teachers tried to work with him, but that didn't work so well either. He was just playing by ear with his left hand because he's a lefty. At a certain point I was able to move him forward by showing him, with great patience, how to play the melody with his right hand and chords with his left hand, and how to find the correct chords. He's very musical. He learned to play by ear.

A few years ago we found a very creative piano teacher. Because of his unique way of working with Daniel, the teacher has gotten him to do things I never dreamed he would do. Daniel always needed to play everything exactly right, just like he heard it in his head, or on the disc. And this teacher actually got him to improvise freely. I'm sure it's because the teacher was totally accepting of Daniel, in a way that I think is much harder for a father to be with a son.

Eliya: Do you spend much time with Daniel now?

Michael: No, he's busy and I'm busy. Also, when we do music stuff his attention span is very short. He'll play a piece, walk around the house and do something else, and then he'll play another piece. Sometimes he will ask me for help in deciphering some chords for a song. I've found more patience and calm to teach him in a way that allows Daniel to learn at his rate, which is slower than mine.

Eliya: Does Daniel carry a label, a specific diagnosis?

Michael: He's unique. He doesn't have a syndrome. He's his own thing. I can describe him in a hundred ways, but it's very hard to pin it down and say what it is exactly.

He's been analyzed by a thousand people. He's had every kind of therapy: One Brain and homeopathy, healing and acupuncture, play therapy and art therapy. You name it, he's been there, but he's never been given a specific label. I say he has "Daniel syndrome."

Eliya: What expectations of Daniel do you have?

Michael: Expectations? I don't know. I'll just see how he develops. My expectations have sort of evolved to trying to be happy with whatever he can do.

After he graduated school, we took him to counseling and they asked me, "What do you want him to do?" I said, "Whatever he can do." His needs are somewhat simple, which is great. He is limited, but he's very happy. He's a happy kid. I call him "kid," but he's a young man.

Eliya: What challenges do you now have with your son?

Michael: He can get very obsessive about nothing. He'll just start talking, and you might ask, "Daniel, what are you talking about?" You can't move him off the track. That's very frustrating. He takes horseback riding lessons. The instructor tells us that sometimes Daniel is great but that sometimes when he insists, "I can't do this; I don't want to do it," he's just out to lunch. That you can't reach him.

I said to the riding instructor, "Please help Daniel to be more aware by saying to him: 'You know, last week you were here and you were riding and you were happy and this week you're not. What's different about this week from last week?'" Daniel also has a personal gym trainer with whom he has trained for years. The gym trainer also tells us that sometimes Daniel is just not there.

Daniel has to develop more awareness of where he's holding and what he's feeling.

In the last few years, he has made great strides in developing self-awareness, to be able to see himself with a bit more perspective. But there is still much work to do so Daniel can develop even more awareness.

Eliya: When Daniel gets stuck and "isn't there," how does that affect you?

Michael: When he gets stuck and begins to obsess about something—although he's doing it less—sometimes I have to tell him, "Daniel, I can't take it anymore. Go to your room, I can't deal with it."

He also has a lot of fear, but he will not recognize that he has fear. That's frustrating. We sent him off to camp in America two years ago and he was very scared. He kept saying, "I don't want to go, it's not fun, I just want to stay in Israel. Camp isn't fun."

He was a kid who had never been away from home. We took him to a disabilities camp in the Catskills where the kids were very low functioning. We stayed there with him for a couple of hours and we didn't think it was very inviting. All of a sudden, Daniel said, "Okay, you can go now." We left him there for six weeks, and he was fine.

The next summer, we found what we thought was a more suitable camp for him, but Daniel announced: "I don't wanna go there. I want to go where I was last year. This new camp is not good for me." We tried to talk to him, but when he's like that there's nobody to talk to and nobody home. We sent him to the new camp anyway, and he loved it. He had the time of his life.

The same thing happens when he gets sick. If he has any kind of illness, he thinks he's never going to get better. We tell him, "Remember you were sick last year and then you got better?" But he can't see it. He lives in his experience of the moment.

We went to pick up Sara's cousin at a bus stop many years ago and she wasn't there. I remember that Daniel got very upset. If something is not the way it should be, he gets so upset. He feels insecure inside, so he needs the world to be very orderly to compensate for his inner tension. His first therapist suggested that we have him repeat over and over again sentences like: "Tragedies don't happen so fast."

Eliya: What do you think is beneath his fear?

Michael: Daniel is missing the basic sense that things are okay. He can get very shaken up by something that wouldn't shake up the average person, and he's always ready for something terrible to happen. For instance, if somebody's sick, he'll say, "Oh, is she going to die?" I think it's part of this tightness that he holds in himself.

In general, it's hard for him to deal with emotions. He almost never cries. I think he has cried only three or four times in his life. He'll laugh inappropriately at something, like when someone dies. That happened when my grandfather and then my parents died.

He has difficulty recognizing emotions, as in: "Oh, now I'm afraid," or "Now I'm sick and not feeling good." He doesn't have a lot of perspective on where he's holding emotionally and so there are limitations on what he understands about himself and others.

Eliya: Tell me about Daniel's recent progress.

Michael: Actually, he is always developing, which is amazing. Physically, he was always a pushover, because he's very short and had a lot of fear. I could squash him easily. He's been working out for years and does some punching and things like that, but then he started taking boxing lessons with a guy in the neighborhood. A few months ago in play, I attacked him, and he really fought back. He just wasn't going to take it, and he laced into me. I had to work hard to get him down. That was new.

He doesn't know how to use a computer, but if somebody sat with him and helped him, I bet that he could figure it out. On the horses, sometimes he can do a really decent job. On his good days, he is quite independent. I've seen him making progress on a lot of fronts. He's always been developing and that's been very wonderful. It's not like he got to a certain place and that's as far as he can go.

Eliya: Tell me how your other children relate to Daniel.

Michael: Sara had a lot of miscarriages after having Daniel. When he was six we adopted twin babies, a boy and a girl. They're fabulous with him. Sometimes, though, they kind of take advantage of him. I might ask them: "Could you guys clean up?!" They'll turn around and say, "Daniel, clean up!" and he'll do it. But mostly, they love him and they protect him. It's great how they're so understanding of him.

I have a good friend who has a daughter with Down syndrome. When we were considering whether or not to adopt the twins, considering all the work involved, our friend said, "Michael, the best thing you can do for Daniel is to adopt those twins." And he was right. I'm sure that a lot of the progress Daniel has made is because of the twins. His brother is a super-athlete who takes Daniel on hikes and always tells him: "You can do this and you can do that." The twins really love him.

Daniel's brother told me that he had been talking with friends, and one of them had said something derogatory about Daniel. My son was incensed and said to his friend, "How can you say that? He's such a pure soul!" The twins are very good with Daniel.

Eliya: What are you looking forward to for Daniel?

Michael: He's has been studying for the last few years in a program that trains adults with disabilities to be caretakers for the elderly. We have seen him at work, and it is truly inspiring to see how beautifully he interacts with the residents in the old age home where he does his field work. He is genuinely giving to society and using his talents to provide a real and valuable service to the people in the home. This is way beyond the menial tasks he performed when he worked at a pizza shop before entering the training program. Daniel will soon be eligible for a certificate that will certify him as trained in a recognized profession. Hopefully this will lead to a salaried position for him.

Eliya: What about Daniel living away from home?

Michael: Earlier this year he moved into in an apartment about ten minutes from here. It is run by the institute which is training him as a caregiver. He lives with eight other adults with disabilities. After the initial adjustments, he is quite happy there. The residents have a counselor who comes to be with them in the evenings and who works with them to enhance their growth and independence. Daniel now does his own laundry and is making good strides in learning about money. It's great that the setup is not merely babysitting, which it often is in these apartments. He is doing really well there.

Daniel has also been taking part in the institute's new program for learning about building and maintaining relationships, which has also been great. We may see the day when he could get married. Overall, we and the institute feel that Daniel is making great progress and will continue to do so for a long time.

Eliya: What a journey you've been on with Daniel.

Michael: Yes, we have. After we adopted the twins, someone said to us, "You two don't have kids, you have projects!"

Eliya: But through it all, Michael, you have maintained your optimism and your faith.

Michael: Daniel is always growing, always doing better, and getting more and more independent. He needs guidance and care, but all things considered, he's a healthy kid and he is blossoming into a fine young man. That keeps me going.

Eliya: Michael, thank you for sharing so much of yourself with me.

2

MARTIN

Three of Martin's boys have a congenital disability affecting their eyes. One of the three is labeled PDD/ADHD, another is ADHD, and the third is a toddler without a label. Martin works full time, yet he is an active team member with his wife in caring for the needs of all five of their children.

Eliya: Tell me about your family.

Martin: We have four boys and a girl. My oldest son is nine and my daughter is four. They are typical children with no difficulties. The other three boys are eight, seven, and two. They were each born with a genetic defect found in the blood, called Hermansky-Pudlak syndrome (HPS). Accompanying HPS is albinism, another genetic defect which is characterized by decreased pigmentation. In our sons' cases, they have little to no pigmentation in their eyes. This form of albinism is referred to as ocular albinism. The lack of pigmentation causes various vision problems. The three boys each have a condition called nystagmus. Their eyes involuntarily move rapidly from side to side. When this occurs it is difficult to focus.

The boys are not albino like most people think of albino: they have pigment in their skin and hair, though their complexions are pale.

Eliya: How do these conditions affect your boys?

Martin: They all have similar characteristics, but each is affected more or less. For example, they have a very poor concept of depth perception and they need to learn that not every surface is flat. They will walk off a top step as if there are no steps. They have great difficulty seeing distance. Probably the distance between us at this table is about as far as they can see. Being in the sun is difficult, of course. They have to wear sunglasses all the time they are outside. With these vision problems it is difficult for them to play games with other children. Without the distance and depth perception it's really hard to see a ball coming at you until it is too late. They have all needed glasses. My third son, Donny, started the last year only able to read

size 72 fonts on the computer. Now

he can read size 28. With expensive prescription glasses and much special vision training his vision has greatly improved.

Generally, however, the health of the boys is good.

Eliya: Were you aware of this genetic condition before you had the boys?

Martin: No. No one in my family or my wife's family was known to have a genetic defect. Before my second son, David, was born we were totally unaware of the possibility of our children having one either.

Eliya: How did you discover the condition?

Martin: When David was a few months old my wife noticed that he was not tracking objects or faces with his eyes. We asked our pediatrician, who directed us to a pediatric ophthalmologist who diagnosed David as having ocular albinism.

Eliya: Did the ophthalmologist also diagnosis the HPS?

Martin: No. We didn't learn about HPS until several years later when extensive genetic testing was done on the whole family. We started out thinking our only concerns were dealing with vision issues.

Eliya: How did you react to learning that your son had a genetic defect affecting his eyes?

Martin: I figured that it was kind of a fluke. Our firstborn son had no problem and like I said, no one else in the family had the defect. We didn't really know what the condition was or its implications.

At the same time it was disappointing. I began to think about the amount of effort and extra care David would require. And then I started to have doubts about David's future. Could he be a doctor or a lawyer? I remember I went to my eye doctor one day for a routine checkup and I mentioned to him that my son had ocular albinism. He said, "I went to medical school with someone with ocular albinism and he became an eye doctor." It sounded like a nice comfortable pat on the back, like, "Your child can still be functional."

Eliya: Did you ever take it personally that your sons had a genetic defect?

Martin: No. We are dealing with recessive genes that may have been around for many generations. It is one of those things that we could never have known about. After we discovered the genetic issues, my wife and I decided to continue having children despite the possibility of the problem reoccuring. We felt that the benefits of having children outweighed the liabilities, despite how difficult it has been.

Eliya: When you heard the diagnosis, how extensively did you educate yourself about it?

Martin: Me, not so much, but my wife did very much. I was working and my wife was at home. Given that her mother was a special-ed teacher, my wife had more interest in learning about it. And my wife also tends to think five steps ahead before we even get there. I didn't think it was good for me personally to look at statistics, to think far off. That way I don't worry so much. Also, you need a balance between a husband and a wife: if you have a person who's a bit more worried, then the other should be a bit less worried; the mix becomes more of a happy medium.

Eliya: Would you say that you and your wife were working together, that you worked as a team?

Martin: We always make decisions together. Even when we disagree we usually try to have a consensus or we try to find someone else to talk it out with, like a medical professional, or whoever is appropriate.

We expanded our team to include my mother-in-law. Given her professional experience she knew how to arrange for the services we were entitled to receive for David. She helped us to fill out all the papers and she lined up the best team of specialists for her grandson.

Eliya: That must have been a big help to you and your wife to have your mother-in-law arrange all the services for you.

Martin: Of course it was. But at the same time, we still had a load on our plate. It's not just that we had to take our child for a few visits to the doctor for routine check-ups and for colds. My wife now needed to be available at home to accommodate the team of service professionals who were coming to our house. And there's also the follow-up and record keeping and making phone calls and appointments. My wife couldn't go out to work. She still doesn't work. She tells people she has a full-time job taking care of her children.

We certainly never expected our career paths to be redirected because our children had disabilities.

But even with all the services for David in place and my wife able to care for him, the timing was such that we were still under a lot of stress.

Eliya: How so?

Martin: We always had in mind to relocate to Israel, and we had thought that after the birth of our second child we would make the move. But now making a move was not so simple. Services were all set up for our son in New York, but we had no concept of how things worked in Israel. Nonetheless, we knew we wanted to move.

We decided to make a pilot trip to Israel to get ourselves as set up as possible. We brought David, of course, and were able to have him evaluated there by professionals. He qualified for special-ed placement. My mother-in-law put us in contact with a former special-ed coordinator in Israel. We met her on our trip and she told us, "Believe it or not, there is a preschool in Jerusalem which especially caters to vision-impaired children." We were blasted away because in America our only option for preschool for visually impaired children was the Helen Keller Foundation. The program is good but for us as religious Jews it presented big challenges: non-kosher food, plus cultural and religious overtones we did not want our child exposed to. We looked forward to David going into this preschool the second we relocated.

While we were very hopeful that our son would get all the attention he needed to help him with his condition, we didn't know that by moving to Israel we would also discover that ocular albinism was a secondary defect which accompanied a potentially life-threatening condition of the blood.

Eliya: What is it you discovered?

Martin: When we finally moved to Israel my wife was expecting our third child. By the time Donny was born, David was well into the program at the preschool for vision impairment. The school helped us tremendously. They explained to us how the Israeli education and social systems work.

They told us all about who the best doctors were. At the time David was receiving all kinds of therapies: special ed, OT, et cetera. We had a door open to people who understood vision impairments. So when the director of the preschool encouraged us to have our newborn's eyes checked out right away, we followed her advice.

Donny was examined by a pediatric ophthalmologist in the hospital shortly after his birth. We discovered that we now had a second son with albinism.

Eliya: You indicated that you were not too upset when you learned that David had ocular albinism; you thought that it was a "fluke." How was it to now have a second son with the same defect?

Martin: It was a mixed blessing. First, we were happy to have another son, but it was much harder now. So much of our time was already being taken up attending to David's needs alone, and now we had Donny with special requirements. Often I would have to adjust my hours at work, sometimes making up hours at strange times. I now had very little free time for myself.

Also we were "just off the boat," having come to Israel only two or three months before. We didn't have our own apartment yet and we were living with someone else.

We didn't speak Hebrew, so it was very difficult to navigate the system. Even with all the experience we had gathered with David we weren't sure it would help us in our new setting with Donny.

Eliya: May we go back to how you learned about the possible serious implications of albinism?

Martin: As David and Donny grew and became more active we began to notice many blotchy bruises on their bodies. It can become a big problem for parents if a doctor or teacher sees bruises on a child's body because bruises may signal child abuse. Professionals are required by law to report to the police or social services any suspicions of child abuse. So we immediately showed the bruises to our pediatrician, who straight away ordered blood tests.

We knew there was a condition called Hermansky-Pudlak syndrome (HPS), which is sometimes present in people with albinism. But before the blotches started to appear we were not aware of HPS affecting our boys. There are several strains of HPS, some of which cause fibrosis [formation of excess connective tissue in an organ]. Fibrosis can be life threatening. To identify the specific strain the boys carried, the lab took blood samples from our entire family, including my wife and me. The samples were sent to a special lab in America for more complex testing. It took almost two years before the lab could isolate the gene which my boys carry. Thank G-d, their HPS gene is a lighter strain without the risk of fibrosis developing.

Eliya: How did you cope for almost two years uncertain if your boys carried a life-threatening blood condition?

Martin: Of course I worried. It was scary to me. I would think: does my child have a disease that he may not survive? The doctors told us that statistically the chances of the boys having a serious strain of HPS were low and that the bruising in itself did not signal a serious condition. Only by genetic testing would we know for certain. Given the doctors' assurances, I don't think we changed how we managed the boys.

Eliya: You had three young children, two with disabilities. You were new immigrants in a country whose system was unfamiliar and whose language you didn't speak. What kind of support were you receiving to help you deal with the stress?

Martin: My wife went to monthly meetings of a mothers' group led by the social worker at David's preschool. I'm close with a few different Rabbis with whom I spoke. One of my Rabbis has a child who is almost blind in one eye. The child constantly walks into walls and doors, and has other issues. Being able to speak to someone who's listening and understands gave me a tremendous amount of support.

Primarily, though, my wife and I were each other's support.

Eliya: May we talk about David?

Martin: Of course.

Eliya: What diagnosis has David been given?

Martin: He's been labeled ADHD [Attention Deficit Hyperactivity Disorder] and PDD [Pervasive Developmental Disorder: a label for individuals who exhibit some signs of autism but not others; most often the focus is on social interaction issues]. But since he has serious vision problems there is not a consensus about the PDD. The focus is on his communication and social interaction.

Eliya: How did you react when you heard that your son was on the autistic spectrum?

Martin: It's scary to think your child is autistic. We knew David was intelligent and we knew he wasn't like a zombie, like when there's no one to speak to. But we were not really sure where to press the button. When you put a person on a spectrum but you can't pinpoint where he is exactly, it's difficult. Labels aren't nice. You can say a child has issues or problems—okay. When you label a child you bury him because once a child gets a label, it sticks.

On the flip side, it does help to know that the problems are in communication because this sets the direction for intervention. Also, since many schools specialize in working with a particular diagnosis it is good to have a diagnosis.

Eliya: What was David's behavior like in the preschool?

Martin: First of all, David wasn't making eye contact or playing with other children. He would also get on all fours and repeatedly hit his head on the floor. He had big welts on his head. This was before his speech was fully developed so he had difficulty communicating.

Eliya: How did you react when you saw your son hitting his head on the floor?

Martin: It was very hard to see my child hurting himself and to look at his bruised head afterwards. There were times when the head banging was non-stop. We were lost as to what to do for him. I used to say that he's nuts, inflicting himself, banging on himself.

He wasn't a mute child, but he didn't have such developed language. He couldn't put his feelings into words to tell us what was bothering him. I thought he was very frustrated and that banging his head helped him somehow to cope; that it was his way of venting.

My wife and I tried to bolster each other and we prayed that we'd find the help David needed. Thankfully he eventually outgrew the head banging and was medicated at age two and a half in order to help control his impulsivity.

Eliya: What program followed the preschool?

Martin: After two years in the preschool we found a small group setting that specialized in speech and language development. We hoped that developing David's speech and language would encourage his socialization.

Although the program was excellent, it really didn't suit one hundred percent of David's needs, so we were back to square one. David stayed only one year in the speech and language program until we finally found a program specifically for children on the autism spectrum.

Eliya: What problems were you looking to solve in the new program?

Martin: Because he wasn't interacting with other children very much and because he was physically weak, he was inactive. As a result of inactivity he wasn't getting the sensory input typical children his age get from running and jumping and playing.

When David was about six years old he still did not interact much with his peers. He spoke mostly to adults. At school, he would often eavesdrop on his teachers' conversations. He once overheard them comment that the bus driver was not doing such a good job. David interrupted the conversation to say: "You know, I think you should give the guy a word or two; give him a piece of your mind a little bit."

In the beginning we all thought it was cute. But we soon realized that while David's behavior was cute and intelligent, it wasn't age appropriate. It's bittersweet. David displayed intelligent behavior, but he was not functioning appropriately as a six-year-old.

He started to have outbursts, screaming strange guttural sounds at the top of his lungs if he didn't like something the teacher did. Also at home. My wife once made spaghetti for dinner and put ketchup on it but David wanted cheese. He screamed: "NO!" And then threw his plate of food on the floor. These fits sometimes occurred a couple of times a day, some lasting up to an hour. At times he would go under a table to scream and rage and wouldn't come out. He also began to rip and destroy things.

Eliya: What impact has David's school environment had on his behavior?

Martin: Fortunately, the two years in the autism program were very good for David. The program developed David's sensory awareness to compensate for what he wasn't getting from other children. Play activity also relieves stress. The program moved David through very detailed activity steps and he responded well to them.

The staff psychiatrist at the program also prescribed Ritalin, which did help to control the head banging and outbursts. But I don't like what else the Ritalin does to him.

Eliya: What don't you like about David taking Ritalin?

Martin: When David takes it he is docile and can pay attention. There's no doubt that without it he cannot function in the classroom. But once the medicine stops working, he's difficult to control.

By nature, David is a very lively child. When children are doing stupid, silly things, he may not participate with them, but he'll sit there on the couch and crack up with them, with a big smile and a hilarious giggle. You know he's enjoying the scene. On the medication it's not David who is there. The medicine makes him very quiet and self-contained, sometimes zombie-like. If you want a good cleaning person, let me know and I'll send David over when he's on his medicine. He'll set your table, mop the floor, and wash the dishes.

It is very hard for me to see David taken over by the medication. I tell my wife this all the time. This is one thing about which my wife and I disagree.

Eliya: What is David's school program now?

Martin: With his social problems he still needs special education but he's too smart to go into a special-ed institution for children with serious learning disabilities. Put a child who has tremendous cognitive capabilities into such an environment and you may suffocate him. So we had to design a program just for him.

We approached the principal of a private school in our neighborhood, and we requested to mainstream David into a regular classroom. As part of the mainstreaming plan we provided a paraprofessional who is with David all the time. We also hired David's former teacher from the autism program to train the paraprofessional to understand how to work with David's unique needs. Very few regular teachers are trained to work with PDD/autistic-like behavior so we felt it necessary to have David's paraprofessional trained and supervised.

Unfortunately that arrangement with the paraprofessional didn't work out as planned so we designed a new plan. David's former teacher conducted small playgroups with David and children from his class. In addition, she started to provide training to one of the school's special-ed teachers, who at the time was also working with David. David's former teacher serves as a private supervisor of his total educational program.

Eliya: What must you do to assist your boys with their vision problems?

Martin: Their vision issues constantly need attention. We have to make sure they have textbooks with large print and which are not too "busy." When there are lots of pictures and text together on a page it can be difficult for them to focus. We ask that they sit where they can see the board. There are many instruments, computers, various technical aids which can help. We have requested of teachers to use only black markers on their whiteboards. The sharper the contrast the easier it is for them to read the words. The albinism won't ever go away; the only question is how you cope with it. So we actively monitor each boy's situation to make sure that the environment fits them and that they have the visual aids they need.

Eliya: What kind of responses have you had from the boys' teachers to their special requirements?

Martin: Generally, very good. In fact, one of the teachers did a phenomenal thing. David was embarrassed to use a magnifying glass that a special vision teacher recommended he use. He would rather sit there and not be able to read than be the only boy to use a magnifying glass in school. So his teacher bought all the children inexpensive magnifying glasses as the prize for the day. And he talked about visual impairment with the children. The teacher's initiative encouraged David to use his magnifying glass. Without my having to ask, another of David's teachers photographed the text and enlarged it on huge papers.

On the other hand, the response has not always been so positive. With thirty-plus children in a class many teachers can't give my boys the attention they need. One teacher wouldn't permit the special vision teacher into the classroom. I think that teacher felt threatened having an adult observe his class. Another teacher gave me the excuse: "Our class is very small; there's not a lot of space."

I once asked a teacher if he would write in a dark color on his whiteboard so the contrast would be easier to see. He said, "To make my students excited and interested I use multi-colored markers. I'm sorry; I understand your son's problem, but I can't meet your request. My first priority is the whole class."

Eliya: What do you do to get the cooperation of teachers?

Martin: I first go to the principal of the different institutions and tell them what kind of help my child needs. I want the principals to understand that the boys require special assistance and it might be necessary to pull the boys out of class to work with a special teacher. Often this means they miss instruction the rest of the class receives. So the boys' academic performance may not be exactly on the level of the class. It is a big challenge because both David and Donny get pulled out of class two or three times a day.

I am very straightforward about my children's problems and needs. I say to teachers: "When I call you and ask you what's going on, I want you to tell me. I don't want to hear how everything is great. I'm not embarrassed to hear the truth and I won't hold it against you. I know my son can be difficult. I want to know how I can help you to help my son be successful in your class." Many teachers are embarrassed and afraid to tell the parents, but we are exactly the opposite.

Eliya: How is the mainstreaming plan for David working out?

Martin: We've gotten a lot of help from the school but David's problems haven't really gotten better. Last year we thought we had a successful year. This year, it's been horrific.

Eliya: What has happened?

Martin: We're not sure why, but it seems like we took one step forward just to take four or five back. David's outbursts continue very frequently. He has started to hit us. But he's small and weak so he doesn't hurt us. David's occupational therapist recently told us that he now has peculiar hand motions. Hand motions and screaming are things that are common in children on the autistic spectrum. And she's scared that David is going in that direction. It's something we have to monitor. He also chews on his clothing. His collars are shredded. We throw out about one article of clothing per week.

I don't know what to do. I feel like an imbecile, telling people that my son eats his clothing. One of David's teachers wanted to make a deal with him, that if he stops chewing his clothing, he'll get a reward. I was embarrassed that a teacher felt the need to take the initiative to approach my son. We can't seem to get David to stop this behavior.

Eliya: What kind of advice are you receiving about how to understand and help David?

Martin: We have started to take David every week to see a child psychologist recommended to us by David's previous school. She is highly thought of by her peers and we are hoping she will be able to tell us why David is behaving this way, and what to do about it. We've asked so many people but no one seems to know why David's behavior has deteriorated.

My wife met with a psychiatrist who suggested that there are two areas in which David needs development: sensory and emotional. Chewing his clothing gives David sensory input. The psychiatrist said that even if we train David to stop chewing his clothing, say for example by putting vinegar on it, then he'll do something else for the sensory input. That's because there is an emotional thing inside of him which is expressed through the chewing or hitting.

Now we're at a point where we really feel very lost. David has regressed so badly.

Eliya: What is your relationship like with David?

Martin: When he's on the medicine, he's super-receptive, super-playful, super-friendly—but you get the sense that it's not David, that it's someone else. By the time I get home David is usually post-medicine and it's difficult to have a relationship with him. For the most part he won't listen to me and just does whatever he wants to do.

Given my work schedule, we don't have so much time together. I try to learn with him or review what he is studying in school. Our learning together used to be a gauge for me of how David was doing in school. But now I can't learn or review with him if I don't catch him on the medicine at the right time.

Eliya: How do you handle not being able to have the kind of relationship with David that you'd like to have?

Martin: It is very difficult to have a child whom I can't connect to and who doesn't seem to want to connect with me. It's not a "relationship." My interaction with David is just a matter of checks and balances. It is not easy with him.

Last night my wife and I said a very true thing. We feel that sometimes we just want to give David a punch in the stomach. On the other hand we want to cry because we see such a cute, cuddly, sweet child right in front of us. We just want to give him a hug.

Eliya: What about your other boys? Does your third son, Donny, carry any other diagnosis besides albinism?

Martin: Yes. Donny also has a label of ADHD, though much less severe than David. We don't think Donny has learning disabilities. We think his problem is really visual, but the ADHD label is for sure. He has problems sitting. He fidgets in his chair. He cannot sit straight. It's very hard to sit with him for more than five or ten minutes.

He goes to a different school than David. Donny's school has a more cognitive, visually oriented approach. We held Donny back this year in first grade because at the end of last year he could not really read. He could make out letters and sounds, but was not at all focused enough to read a full sentence. In reading comprehension he wasn't even close to being on level.

Eliya: What special assistance does Donny receive?

Martin: He requires visual aids like the magnifying glass for reading. He also uses a book stand so printed material is presented to him at a particular angle which lines up with his eyes. Donny carries a big bag with him to school every day, in which he has the book stand and all his books.

A private teacher takes him out of the classroom at least once a day. A different special-ed teacher works with him two days a week.

Eliya: How does Donny interact with others?

Martin: Very well, even though Donny has a word-retrieval problem. He knows what he wants to say, but he can't always come up with the word, so he'll say, "Can we go to the ummm, ummm, ummm...you know, that place where we went to last time which was really exciting?"

Eliya: You have a third son with ocular albinism.

Martin: Yes, our baby. He's two years old. So far he's doing okay.

Eliya: How do your other children get along with David and Donny?

Martin: We're having a problem with our oldest son, Jonathan. He has a very hard time with David. For pretty much the whole last year we took Jonathan to a psychologist because he was exhibiting aggressive behavior; he was unhappy. The psychologist said that he has a lot of baggage. Jonathan won't sit next to us in synagogue. He says that everybody knows about David's behavior and it embarrasses him very much. Jonathan didn't want David to be in the same school with him. Sometimes they fight, and since Jonathan is bigger than David, Jonathan lets him have it.

Is Jonathan angry? Maybe anger that comes from embarrassment or frustration. David's outbursts and screaming are particularly difficult for Jonathan. We try to quiet David but often he just keeps on going.

The other children are young and get along okay.

At home David sometimes participates in family activities, especially a card game he likes to play. But mostly he plays by himself with a few Lego-like pieces which he lines up in a straight line. Then he lies on the floor and makes truck and car sounds. He's in his own world playing with trucks and buses.

Eliya: What you are describing sounds like typical family interaction. What is it really like in your house with three boys requiring so much attention?

Martin: Sometimes it is quite typical, but other times it definitely is not. David tears the house apart when he gets frustrated. We've had to lock all the doors in our house including the bathrooms. He goes into the bathrooms and empties out the shampoo and soap bottles. If we didn't lock all the doors, his lack of self control could result in complete disruption to the house and everything in it. If he wants something to eat or drink he raids the kitchen and opens up packages. Recently he has been taking bottles from the refrigerator and drinking directly from the bottle.

Two nights ago my wife and I were eating dinner together after feeding all the children and he bops into the kitchen, takes his hand and shoves it into the pot of food, and grabs himself a little dessert. Being the second oldest child, David models very bad behavior to his younger siblings.

Eliya: How does David get along in the community outside of school?

Martin: It isn't so easy. In the synagogue David frequently goes behind the curtains in front of the ark which houses the Torah scrolls. He then opens up the ark to see what's inside. He does this during the time when everyone in the synagogue is praying.

When David prays he screams at the top of his lungs. He also has a hand motion and a bizarre sound that he makes. It's like announcing: "Hello, I'm here. Everybody pay attention!" One of the leaders of the congregation approached me and said: "During prayers your son walks around on the platform in the middle of the synagogue and it bothers people. If it's at all within your ability to stop your son, I'd really appreciate it." I give this person a lot of credit for the way he approached me. I understand that certain things bother people. Although it's no secret, and people know that my child has difficulties, this time I was really embarrassed. Even when I do take him, if he starts acting inappropriately and I tell him to come to me, he won't. There are certain times I just have to carry him home physically or hold his hand forcefully to get him to leave. I'm not sure if I can take my son to the synagogue anymore.

Eliya: How do you feel about the reactions of people to David?

Martin: My wife and I are embarrassed. It's difficult for us, especially since we live in a religious community which has well-defined rules and expectations for people to walk on a straight and narrow path. For example, chewing gum relaxes David and gives him sensory input which helps him to focus. That said, we didn't even ask the principal if David can chew gum. His response would surely be: "Children don't chew gum in school. It's not allowed and not acceptable. There's nothing to talk about." I know he wants to help me, but he just can't. He's an administrator of a big school. There are certain policies and regulations which they have to follow.

A close friend of ours heard from her neighbor that in school children make fun of how David looks. Indeed, David's hair is very curly and all over the place. This neighbor didn't have the courage to tell us outright, so she did it in an indirect way. My wife was very sad to hear this, but at least consoled somewhat that someone cared about us enough to mention it.

Eliya: How is it for you to be known as a family with so many children with special needs?

Martin: We're very open about all the problems the boys have. We have met other parents of children with special needs who are very closed...you know, everybody has their own calculations. When your children have vision impairment, people see it. There's nothing to hide about it. Exactly the opposite. Donny is the only one in school who takes a book stand to class. It's okay; everyone knows that he has a visual problem.

Eliya: How do you react when you see David accomplish tasks typical children accomplish?

Martin: David does not go out to play at recess. He's very self-absorbed. Which is part of the problem. I feel very sad for David because he doesn't experience the fun things that most children do. So when he does do something "typical" I am really happy.

We were in the park near us, and even though David is physically weak and generally scared of physical challenges he went up and down a tall ladder. He did the monkey bars a few months ago. He was never in his life able to do monkey bars. These were big accomplishments for him.

There are ups and downs. On the one hand, I am so happy with the achievements that he makes. They're achievements which, for him, are way, way beyond.

Eliya: If you are comfortable telling me, what does it cost you to provide the special assistance your children receive?

Martin: With his PDD diagnosis David is entitled by the national insurance program to disability compensation, which covers about half of his costs. In addition, he gets private teaching assistance from the municipality. From the Ministry of Education he is eligible for placement in special-ed schools, but we've chosen not to put him there.

So far, the other boys are not eligible for disability compensation, though Donny gets supplementary help in school with a teacher trained to work with vision impairments. His teacher is also provided by the municipality.

Out of pocket, I pay for David's trainer/supervisor, his afternoon sensory program, and a psychologist he sees weekly and whom we consult with every month. I also pay for the boys to go to what we call "morning exercises." It is work to further develop their sensory awareness. It also helps to relieve tension. Donny gets one-on-one occupational therapy twice a week which I pay for as well as twice-a-week afternoon group therapy.

Then there are glasses for the boys, medications which are only partially subsidized, and various vision aids. Their glasses are nonstandard prescription, custom-order lenses, which are quite expensive. To top it off, the lenses have to be transition lenses which automatically become shaded in the sun, adding even more to the expense. Being boys, someone's frames are always breaking, requiring us to purchase outright a few extra frames just in case.

It's a significant amount, believe me.

Eliya: What kind of a support system do you have besides the two of you?

Martin: Our parents are very much involved. My mother-in-law is a widow and lives here in Jerusalem. When she comes over she spends time with David. One thing she does is brush his arms with a soft brush. This is an activity recommended to develop David's sensory awareness. My wife and I rarely get a free moment to do this with David at home. So it's a big help. Besides speaking on the phone with my family who live in America, we don't have too much more of a support system.

Eliya: From where do you draw your strength, Martin?

Martin: Sometimes I don't know. For certain, I do feel that G-d is looking out for us. It's not easy; it's very frustrating. I'm not sure what keeps me going. We think about our kids, but we don't think about ourselves so much. If that's good or it's not good, I can't say for sure, but that's how it is.

Eliya: What are your big challenges now?

Martin: What's the hardest for me right now is that we felt that we were getting somewhere with David, but his behavior has regressed and now we feel lost. When you invest a lot of energy and effort into something and. you feel you're achieving some goals, then in the end, you can give a huff and say, "It was worth it." But now the investment does not seem to be paying off.

We had a meeting last year about David with his case coordinator and his teacher. His teacher reported, "David is great; he's a good child," and we were sitting there and asked, "Does he have any outbursts?" And the teacher said, "No." And what about this and that? Again: "No." And my wife and I were smiling at each other. We thought we were at the wrong meeting. This is not our son. It was like a dream come true. I was about to cry.

But when things started regressing we started to feel very lost again. And the channels that we are going through—we don't have a car, we can't drag people to appointments and go see so many different doctors, and even if we could, David has school. We can't just take them to doctors all day. Part of my son being normal is doing what normal children do. If my child gets taken out of class every day then, of course, he's not going to be a normal child with a normal school experience.

One of the difficulties we have is that we speak to a bunch of people; some we ask for advice, some we don't ask, but they give it anyway. Sometimes we need to gently tell people, "Will you just leave us alone for a little bit?" Maybe we just spent a whole day on this, going to doctors or therapists, and could use some quiet and change of scenery.

My wife and I say that we may not do everything our kids need. There comes a point in time, my wife says to me: "Physically I can't do it anymore. I can't go see another doctor. I'm sorry, I can't. I just don't have it in me. We're trying our best, doing whatever's within our capabilities."

But there comes a point where we say, "Enough."

Eliya: Have you ever questioned why you have so many challenges?

Martin: No. Although I pray every day that I should have the physical and emotional capability to provide my children what they need. With all of the challenges our children present, we look at our children as gifts.

Eliya: What does having had your children with their challenges done for you personally?

Martin: I appreciate life more. I see my children who, despite having difficulties, are still able to do what they do and I say to myself: Wow, it's amazing what a person can do. I see these accomplishments and cannot understand how some people will tell me I shouldn't have children because they may have serious difficulties.

I also believe that my marriage is stronger, because my wife and I have been through a lot. So I like to hope and think that we're very supportive of each other.

Being a father to my children has developed my sense of giving. I'm not able to be so self-absorbed anymore.

I have much more appreciation for teachers and staff. When I compare the effort the teachers of David make to teach him to the effort required to teach any of the other boys, whatever their needs, I am very impressed. I am grateful to all my sons' teachers, but especially to David's. And I have a debt of gratitude till today to the school that accepted David.

One thing, in particular, that I have learned from David is to appreciate when times are good. Unfortunately, it's often only in hindsight when times are bad that I remember that there are also good times. It is very important to remember the good.

Eliya: Thank you, Martin, for sharing so openly with me.

POSTSCRIPT

About six weeks after giving this interview, Martin's wife gave birth to their sixth child and their second girl. Given the family history, within a few hours of birth the baby was examined by a pediatric ophthalmologist. The doctor confirmed a diagnosis of HPS and albinism.

Martin emailed to me the following:

"Happy as we were upon the new birth, we couldn't keep the news from dimming the happiness, even just a bit. Still, as with our other children, we try to be optimistic and look towards a bright future. It is our hope and prayer, that the One who gave us the strength and courage to face all the challenges we have had until now, will continue to watch over us and our children, including our new daughter, to help them grow and bring happiness to all those around them."

3

BEN

After having five daughters, Ben finally had a son. All of Ben's expectations for who his son might become were shattered when he learned that the baby had Down syndrome. Jacob is a young man now, but Ben still wonders what life might have been like if his son had been born "typical."

Eliya: Please tell me about your son.

Ben: Jacob is in his late twenties, has Down syndrome. Great kid. Wonderful. We love him. When he's not around, we miss him. He lives at home, goes to work at a sheltered workshop in Jerusalem. I take him in the morning. My wife generally picks him up unless it's a problem. He's there every day.

We located the workshop program pretty quickly when we relocated to Israel seven years ago, and Jacob has been there ever since. We're very happy. It's working well. Everyone there wears black and white, but he comes with his baseball T-shirt and cap, or whatever, and they love him. They couldn't be nicer.

Eliya: You had an important community position when you lived in America. Did you ever feel the need to defend your son in your community?

Ben: Never. My wife did advocate for a time in the local Jewish day school to create a program for our son, but it didn't meet with a whole lot of success for many different reasons. We didn't want to send him to public school, but there was no choice.

Eliya: What was your son's school setting prior to the move?

Ben: Where we lived, Jacob started out in the local Jewish day school. He was there with the aid of a shadow. As Jacob aged and developed, there was, unfortunately, no Jewish setting there which could deal with his situation. So we placed him in a public school where he was mainstreamed. After completing public school, Jacob worked some in city-run sheltered workshop programs.

Eliya: I've spoken with fathers who have faced serious challenges to the family's lifestyle when their child is in a public school setting. How did you deal with that?

Ben: Before my son entered public school my wife and I were very concerned about the lifestyle difference. It was not our first choice that he be there, and we did consider leaving that community. I looked for a position in other cities which had Jewish schools for our son, but it just never worked out.

I can recall when I applied for one position and it didn't work out, I remember feeling crushed—not so much because of me; I very happy where I was. The interviewing elsewhere was more for Jacob because we knew that if he could attend a Jewish day school suited to his needs, he would be better off.

But we bounced back. To be honest, looking back, given our son's mental ability, I don't know how much we or he missed by not being in a day school.

As it turned out, the school where Jacob went was very, very good. His teachers and the administration were so incredibly accommodating that they couldn't do enough for us and for him. They acknowledged and accepted that he was Jewish and religious.

Also, it was a short day so he was home early every day. OK, when the holiday season came around he heard about Santa Claus. It wasn't such a big deal. But other than that, there were no other issues and, besides, he was getting plenty of Jewish training at home. He's a social kid and had Jewish social outlets, so he wasn't especially influenced in a negative way at all.

Eliya : Was the move to new surroundings with a foreign language challenging for Jacob in any way?

Ben: No. Thank G d, it was a good settling in, as they say.

Eliya: How has Jacob reacted to his workshop program here?

Ben: Very happy fellow. Never complains.

Eliya: Describe his skills to me.

Ben: Every kid with Down syndrome plays out differently. I think Jacob is medium-functioning. He couldn't take a bus by himself. He doesn't have that sort of focus. Typical of Down syndrome, he's not analytical in any sense, but he has an incredible memory for things. He loves to listen to Jewish music.

Since most Jewish music takes words from the Bible, he knows many verses which he remembers. He has more of a visual memory than an analytical one. If you ask him simple things in math, unless he memorizes it, he doesn't have the ability to figure it out.

He listens to music in his free time. Also he'll open up the Bible and just read from the text. He can read Hebrew and English. Sometimes he'll write it out. He likes to write, likes to copy things, but he writes with difficulty because the dexterity in his wrists is very, very poor.

Eliya: How is his health?

Ben: He has celiac. Before the diagnosis it was very frightening because Jacob went into seizures from a lack of calcium in his blood. We didn't understand why until the diagnosis of celiac was made. Thank G-d, we caught it right away and learned to keep him away from foods containing gluten.

He also has problems with the bones in one wrist and in his legs. The doctors did surgery on his feet and he has splints, but on his hand they said it was too difficult. The fusion of the bones was such that they didn't think surgery could help. So Jacob doesn't have flexibility in that wrist, which leads to certain situations where he needs help, like putting on shoes and buttoning buttons.

He can't walk very quickly, can't really run, although he did walk in the Jerusalem Marathon. In that marathon we walked with him and we all had a great time.

Even though we're very careful about what he eats because of the celiac, we recently saw that he was putting on some extra weight. Even though he's not heavy, my wife got him started working out on the treadmill. He walks a few miles a day and has lost about eight or nine pounds.

But other than the celiac and his physical mobility, thank G-d, he's fine.

Eliya: What kind of social outlets does Jacob have?

Ben: He's involved with an organization for individuals with disabilities. He's been on some retreats with the group. The people there are really great.

At work, everyone loves him and he loves to go there. When Jacob has an appointment or some other reason that prevents him from going to work he definitely is not happy. Other than his work environment or an organization event, it's just us and the extended family, when we get together. At times my brother comes to town, as do other relatives, just like any other family.

Eliya: What number is Jacob in the lineup of your children?

Ben: He's the last one. After five girls, he's the boy.

Eliya: What was it like for you? After five girls you finally have a boy and he has Down syndrome.

Ben: It was difficult. It took a period of adjustment. But thank G-d, it wasn't a long period.

I experienced a mixture of emotions. One was guilt, like: "What did I do? Perhaps I did something wrong. After five girls, why shouldn't I have a healthy son?" It was a feeling of guilt, but I began to ask myself: *"Guilt for what?"* I couldn't pinpoint anything specific, like: "Did I do something wrong to deserve this?"

There was a little bit of embarrassment. What are people going to think of me? Not that I felt guilty myself, but perhaps other people might think I was in some way at fault. But again, that period was very, very short-lived. When I say short-lived, I mean like in a week or two it was gone.

I was able to deal with it. But at the beginning, it did hit me. I just had to pull myself together and understand it for what it was.

Eliya: What particularly challenged you?

Ben: How do you explain it to people, what do you say to your kids? That was an issue: how do we tell the girls about it? The birth took place on Friday, so my wife and I decided we weren't going to say anything until after the Sabbath ended.

Each one of the girls handled it differently. They called their friends, then little by little the community heard about it and fortunately there was a Rabbi in the community whose child also had Down syndrome, so it wasn't an unfamiliar situation to anyone.

Eliya: In those first two weeks when you were trying to sort out your reactions to having a boy with Down syndrome, what helped you?

Ben: My wife and I were on the same page. The girls were on the same page. No one said something like, "Well, maybe you should put the child in a home." That never came up. When our respective parents heard about it, they couldn't have been more supportive. In fact, when we decided to name him after my grandfather and my wife's grandfather, I asked our parents: "How you feel about naming him after the grandfathers?" They immediately agreed. There wasn't any hesitation over the phone. That the parents on both sides were supportive made a big difference. For them the Down syndrome issue was no issue at all.

How they personally dealt with it, I have no idea. I never asked them. I wasn't interested in finding out. Because even if they did have a problem with it, they never in any way related to us about it other than with compassion and support. Everyone has to deal with challenges like ours in his own way, privately.

Eliya: And your wife, as you recall, how was she handling it?

Ben: At first, Becky was devastated, but soon, much like myself, it was all about going forward. "What do we have to do? Let's find out how to do it." We immediately got involved with organizations in town. We began to find out what to do very quickly, because the hospital staff were very helpful. And everywhere we went, everyone was very supportive and ready to assist us.

I cannot remember, even once, whether it was a person or an institution, or anybody, who made us feel uncomfortable, making us feel like we were outsiders.

Eliya: You had already been a father five times, but did you have any idea what to expect about raising a child with Down syndrome?

Ben: No. We didn't know what to do at the beginning. But then we had people, like the other couple in town, who also had a child with Down syndrome. They were the first phone call my wife made. And after a long silence, the mother said, "I can only wish you the joy we have from our son." They came to visit us in the hospital. Their son was in his preteens at that time. They said to us, "Don't worry, we're here. We'll tell you what to do."

Eliya: Was it a challenge to you as a man to be in a situation where you didn't know what to do?

Ben: I can't recall ever feeling like that. When I'm faced with difficult situations, I try to figure out where to go, what to do and whom to ask. This became another very momentously challenging situation, but I knew that there were answers out there. People told us there were. We weren't reinventing the wheel.

I remember that we discovered a journal about Down syndrome which we subscribed to, and we got information from there. I'm the one that started reading up on it. That's my way. My wife is more practical, but I wanted to know what it was all about, so I read a few books on the subject. This was before Internet. I wanted to know what Down syndrome was and try to make sense of it all so I could put everything in perspective.

Eliya: How did your life change being the parent of a child with disabilities?

Ben: Your life changes in certain practical ways. The daily routine changes. Even now, we can't leave him alone. We're used to it already, but in the beginning it was challenging.

He always needed help getting dressed, getting undressed, going to the bathroom. It's almost like dealing with an infant when you have to do everything for him. But in Jacob's case even in those areas of getting dressed, going to the bathroom, showers, stuff like that, it just continues indefinitely. It's not a big deal; it becomes part of your day.

Eliya: How did having Jacob in the family impact on family relationships?

Ben: Nothing changed as far as relationships, thank G-d. In fact, Jacob being in the family has brought us closer together. For years, everyone knew Jacob needed help, so everyone chipped in. Becky always learns the weekly Bible portion with Jacob, so we'd make a big deal when he'd finish his learning. And all the girls would chime in. We'd make a big deal about him, like at a birthday. Everyone felt that they wanted to be a part of his life.

Eliya: How does your son get along with others?

Ben: Down syndrome children are very, very friendly. But sometimes they're so friendly they are in your face. They'll hug you too much, they'll literally physically push you—not, G-d forbid, to harm you, but just to relate to you in their own way. Jacob is not that way at all. He's very loveable, but he's not one who goes around hugging people. He'll ask for your name, and ask, "How are you?" and if you ask him how he is he'll say, "Thank G-d." He's a very talkative, friendly person. In the synagogue, he walks around and says to people, "Oh, how do you do? Welcome." Except for the fact that he talks slowly and his speech is sometimes slurred, you'd think he's just a very friendly guy. Everyone loves him. If someone gets an honor in the synagogue, he congratulates them on being honored. Loudly.

He's such a wonderful, really loveable kid, that as he grew older you simply wanted to be around him.

Eliya: How does Jacob participate in family activities?

Ben: It is really something to see him at the Sabbath meal table. He chimes in, he starts singing songs. He sings all the Sabbath songs. I ask him questions about the weekly Bible portion and he enjoys giving an exposition of a concept that he has learned. We talk about anything and everything. He has these routines that he acts out; he's very funny.

Eliya: With whom does your son have a closer relationship, you or your wife?

Ben: One is not closer than the other. We each have a different relationship. My wife takes care of his immediate needs. She prepares his food, dresses him in the morning, at night. She takes care of those kinds of things.

I'm more of the guy type of thing. I'll say: "Let's play ball or take a walk together." We talk, we fool around. On Friday we like to learn particulars of Jewish law together.

That's how it has played out. My wife is more of a nurturer. And I'm the more playful sort of person.

Eliya: Does Jacob have any special names that he calls you, endearing sort of terms?

Ben: For me, no. For his sisters he has different nicknames. "Big D" for Debbie, who's the oldest. Things like that. But we're just Mommy and Daddy.

Eliya: Did all his sisters get involved with him in equal ways?

Ben: Until they married and moved out of the house, they did. They always wanted to help us. If we wanted to go out, they'd babysit. Things like that. We have one unmarried daughter in the house, and she is a great help.

Eliya: If I may, Ben, a more personal question. Did you ever feel disappointed that your only son was not typical?

Ben: Yes, in the beginning I had been hoping for a son and that the dreams I had for him would be realized. To be honest, I'd have to say that there are still times, very, very few, like maybe twice a year, I'll say to myself, "Hmm... Jacob is twenty-some-odd years...I wonder what sort of person he would be if he were normal." Nothing more than that.

I didn't even think about it, until you asked. I don't obsess about it. I don't get depressed about it. I just fantasize a bit: "I wonder what he might be doing with his life, maybe this or that..." This thought goes on for maybe sixty seconds, and then, it's over.

Eliya: What do you think about the future for Jacob?

Ben: We have thought about the issue of his care after we're gone. We have to arrange for who is going to take care of Jacob when we're not around (may we live and be well to 120). We began thinking about that once we got to a certain age. Which one of his sisters would care for her brother? We're certainly not going to send him to a home. That might work for other boys like him, but not for our son.

We think about Jacob's financial needs. We don't want him to be a burden, so we have to plan for that. Everyone does it in their own way. A special account, or a trust.

These are certainly not pleasant matters to consider, but I mention them because there's a point when every parent needs to think about these things.

Eliya: How have you and your wife worked together to provide for Jacob's needs?

Ben: My wife has pretty much been the stalwart person in taking care of Jacob, much more than me.

It's true that I prepared him for reading the Bible portion for his bar mitzvah [a Jewish boy's initiation into adulthood at age thirteen] and for his speech, but Becky taught him initially how to read Hebrew. She deserves the real credit. Becky would always read to the girls before they went to sleep. It was a nightly ritual. She would read a variety of books to them. And, of course, she would read to Jacob as well. No different. Every night on schedule to this day, she reads to him. I only fill in when she's not home.

Thanks to Becky my son loves books. Quite often he reads books on his own. I don't know how much he understands, but he can actually read the books quite well.

Eliya: What kept you from teaching him?

Ben: It was hard for me to do that on a consistent basis because of my job. It made it very difficult. My wife is very much into consistency. And I couldn't always be consistent, but it was never a problem or an expectation of me. Sort of like a division of labor.

Eliya: So you and your wife work as a team.

Ben: Oh yes. Absolutely. Never an issue. Becky knew that anytime she needed me to do something I was available. And I knew she wouldn't ask me unless it was important, so if she did ask me, I would drop everything. And I would try never to burden her with other family needs when her time and involvement with Jacob needed to come first.

Things happened sort of naturally. It wasn't like we sat down with a piece of paper to make assignments. We were on the same page from the get-go. I'm very grateful. I have a wonderful wife.

Eliya: What have you discovered about yourself as a result of raising your son?

Ben: Patience. As the Talmud says, you may not be able to see how it's all going to come together, but eventually, it does.

At Jacob's bar mitzvah I shared my wife's interpretation of the prayer we say after eating most foods: *"The One Who creates numerous living things with their deficiencies..."* With a child with Down syndrome you learn to appreciate small things, all the little successes he has achieved, these little mini-achievements. You learn to appreciate and value them.

It is amazing how measuring up to the challenge of raising Jacob has generalized to other things. I'm sure my wife would agree that we're all better people having had to adjust, accommodate, and change because we have a child with Down syndrome. I'm convinced of it.

Eliya: I have read that there are opinions held by our great Rabbis which suggest that the souls of children with Down syndrome are pure and that they have done all the spiritual correcting they need to do. If so, what would that imply about whom your son is in the world for, himself or for you?

Ben: That's an interesting question, and the short answer is that he's here for us, not for himself. He's here for you and me. How we respond to someone like Jacob says something about ourselves. It's funny. I had a Sabbatical in '96–'97, right before Jacob's bar mitzvah.

I had several questions about the legal status of my son according to Jewish law. The answers to my questions would determine whether I should prepare Jacob for a traditional bar mitzvah. The Rabbi I consulted met Jacob a number of times. The Rabbi concluded that Jacob's intelligence was sufficient to fulfill the bar mitzvah requirements like any typical bar mitzvah boy. So I went ahead with the bar mitzvah preparations.

Eliya: How did Jacob relate to the Rabbi?

Ben: With Jacob you could be the biggest Rabbi in the world, and my son would say to you: "Hello. How are you?" He cuts through the distance between people and "breaks the ice" in the nicest of ways. He's that sort of kid.

Eliya: We should all be like that.

Ben: That's the point. When you see Jacob behave that way, no pretenses, just plain, pure, genuine emotion, you just love him because that's really who he is. Completely genuine to the core. He hasn't changed much from when he was younger. That same innocence, it's still there. Which is remarkable. He hasn't become corrupted or cynical. He hasn't outgrown that childlike spirit which amazes and excites all of us. He hasn't become jaded or bored with his life. He loves his life and is happy and content.

Eliya: What do you look forward to for Jacob?

Ben: If we have one concern now, it's that we want to keep him as healthy as possible and see that his needs are taken care of. That's it, that's our concern. Other than that, we don't expect him to be anything more than what he is.

Eliya: Do you feel as though you yourself have done enough for your son?

Ben: I guess if I would ask myself that question, I would say probably if I pushed myself more, I could learn with him more. Like, I say to him, "Do you want to learn now?" and he'll sometimes say, "Well...later." I have so many other things to do, so that when he says no, I don't push as much. I guess that's my one regret, the only thing I can think of over the years that I could have pushed more. I don't think Jacob would have objected if I had. But more recently I've been trying to learn with him, and hopefully it will continue.

In every other sphere, I think we've done and are doing whatever we can.

Of course, there's always more you can do, but I really think we are blessed. I think my son has made a tremendous difference in our lives. My wife and I both, and all of our children, are very grateful. And even when those stray thoughts intrude, like: "I wonder what he could have been like...," we immediately reflect on how we would be missing all of these incredible experiences with our son. And in the grand scheme of things, who's to say which is more precious?

Eliya: Thank you, Ben, for sharing so much about yourself and Jacob with me.

4

ELAZAR

When Dovid was seven and a half, he, several siblings, and his father, Rabbi Elazar Grunberger, were in a major car accident. In one instant, Dovid went from being a Little League superstar and "A" student to a brain-damaged child who has had to relearn how to swallow. Rabbi Elazar has never given up on Dovid making a full recovery.

Eliya: Tell me what Dovid was like before the accident.

Elazar: Dovid was always very, very popular in school and a great ball player. At age seven he regularly played hardball with the twelve-year-olds and he was the shortstop in Little League. He was also a tremendous student in both religious and secular studies.

Eliya: What does Dovid remember about his life from before the accident?

Elazar: I don't know what are real memories or what he knows from what we have talked about with him. We were recently back in St. Louis for the first time since we moved to Israel, in September 2011. It was very interesting for me to see that Dovid was able to recall a lot of things from the past...his friends, the house.

Eliya: Describe more of Dovid before the accident.

Elazar: As the youngest of ten children, he was very cute and sweet. My wife and I, and all his siblings, always related to him as the youngest child. He was a kid who really didn't know how to walk because he was usually running everywhere. He might have been a little ADHD, but at such a young age, it was too early to tell.

Before the accident, he was doing well in school. We still have his test papers showing 100s in whatever he was learning. Just before the accident his brother began to learn with him some advanced textual material, but Dovid didn't have a chance to get very far.

He was very confident and skilled on his roller blades and his two-wheeler. But baseball was his favorite sport, whether it was playing catch or going to his Little League games. It was always wonderful to watch him.

Eliya: Tell me about the accident.

Elazar: We were on a family outing on holiday. A good friend of ours had a farm with horses on hundreds of acres, about an hour and fifteen minutes away from St. Louis. This friend built a swimming pool, kept golf carts, and had any toy you could possibly think of. We were riding the horses, and Dovid was on the carts and swimming like a fish in the pool.

When we ready to leave, my wife, my son-in-law, my daughter, and a few others went in one car, about fifteen minutes before us. We were in the other car—three sons, two daughters, and myself. One of my daughters was driving. I was in the front seat and must have dozed off.

The next thing I knew, I was awake. We were upside down, or on the side, whatever it was, and my daughter who was driving was crying and screaming at me to wake up. I pulled myself together and got the seat belts off. The paramedics were already there, so I don't know how long I was unconscious.

I was told that ambulances were coming, as were helicopters to airlift us to four different hospitals.

Eliya: What did you do in those first moments after regaining consciousness?

Elazar: When they were trying to drag me out, I just remember that I said, "How are my kids?" The paramedic said, "Well, they're all crying and screaming, so that's a good sign."

I prayed: "You know, G-d, they're Your kids too." I was helpless. Somehow, I can't remember how, while in the car I texted, emailed, or called a friend of mine, Boruch Rabinovitz, who runs Aish HaTorah Yeshiva [yeshiva is a place for advanced studies in Jewish text] in Manhattan. I said, "Send an email to the Aish HaTorah email list. Give them my kids' names. We were in a serious auto accident and I need everyone's prayers."

Prayers started going all over the world as the message was forwarded from one place to another. My son Moishe was married about a year, and he was in Jerusalem. He organized a gathering of about forty or fifty people at the Western

Wall, mostly people from St. Louis who were in Israel. All over the world, people were praying for us.

Eliya: It's amazing that your first reaction was to seek prayer. What condition were you in?

Elazar: They say I had a concussion.

Eliya: What was Dovid's condition?

Elazar: They didn't tell me that my son Dovid was injured the most, and the others were also pretty well injured. That night a friend picked me up at the hospital where I had been taken and he drove me to the hospital where Dovid was. My wife and people from the community were already there. Dovid was in neurosurgery, where the doctors were trying to alleviate swelling around his brain.

At the scene of the accident medics had found Dovid unconscious and had done CPR. It wasn't certain if he would pull through. They were just trying to do what they could to save his life.

Eliya: How did you react to the news of Dovid's condition?

Elazar: We were in the hospital, waiting. I don't know if it was denial, but I just felt it would be okay. I thought: *Even if you have to go to the hospital, you heal and you come out okay.* I was never in a situation like this before.

My positive emotional and psychological response at that point was different than it might have been ten, fifteen, or twenty years ago. I'm not saying that I'm more insensitive or more callous, but I'm saying that there's a certain level where age brings an understanding that we have to bounce back and do the best we can under the circumstances.

Eliya: Do you know what the circumstances were that caused the accident?

Elazar: It was something that could happen to anybody. My daughter did not see a stop sign. I don't know of anyone who has a driver's license who hasn't ever actually missed a stop sign.

Eliya: It must have been so very difficult for your daughter as the driver of the car. How did you help her to deal with the natural reaction to blame herself?

Elazar: Today she's strong and very resourceful, but it took her time to realize that she couldn't call it her fault. Matter of fact, I've had a hard time calling it an accident. There are no accidents.

Here she was in the open country at an intersection with two cars coming together at the exact same second. It would have never happened if we had left twenty seconds before or twenty seconds later, or if we had been traveling at a different speed limit. It's just that G-d has a master plan; we know that intellectually, but it's a matter of living with it. It's so clear that this was a master plan and completely not in our hands.

No one wishes this upon anyone and no one wants this to ever happen, and yet it happened. You just say, "Okay, so how are we going to live with it and deal with it?" Some things are bigger, more obscure, or more difficult to come to terms with.

Those three years post-accident were very difficult for her. Thank G-d, she had, and has, a very strong group of friends. She was young then, but grew and matured through therapy and working on herself. She's now studying to be a therapist, and I believe she'll be the most awesome therapist around when she gets that degree.

Eliya: The accident must have changed your home life dramatically.

Elazar: I had always tried to be helpful in the home, but obviously this new reality required a lot more help. It was a whole game changer—to the point where we describe the family as pre-accident and post-accident. There were now appointments and such things, and it required a different kind of lifestyle. But at the same time, you carry on with your work and whatever you have to do.

Eliya: What was it like for Dovid after the accident?

Elazar: It has always been intense. The first few weeks Dovid was in intensive care. From the ICU he was in step-down, a transition period between ICU and normal in-patient care. Then to rehab. Following four months in the hospital he went to an outpatient rehab hospital for six months. And then it was part-time in school, where he was wheelchair bound.

For the first six months after the accident, he lost his ability to swallow so he was fed by a G-tube (gastric tube). When we brought him home, we had to learn how to use the machinery for the G-tube and put the right formulas in.

Then, when he started learning how to swallow again, we had to be careful that he shouldn't aspirate. I remember it was during Passover, six months after the accident, he was eating puree. For chewing, it would take around twenty-two minutes for his brain to click into gear to remember how to chew and swallow.

I remember that he went with the G-tube to Camp Simcha Special (in New York), which is an amazing place. We took the G-tube out on the day before Rosh Hashanah, the Jewish New Year. So it was almost a full year that he had it in, but he was already eating. Now he has a great appetite, and he can swallow pills better than adults can. He just puts them in his mouth and swallows. No water.

Eliya: It is hard to imagine what it must have been like to watch your child having to relearn how to swallow and chew.

Elazar: I had to see him in diapers for I can't remember how long. It was probably two years after the accident before he regained complete control.

Eliya: What kind of assistance does Dovid require today?

Elazar: He cannot dress himself because he doesn't have use of his left hand, so we need to help him deal with buttons. He has elastic pants which are easier for him to deal with. If you ever tried to use just one hand getting dressed, it's a very difficult thing to do, so he needs assistance with that.

I remember when the occupational therapist came, maybe six months after the accident, to show him how to brush his teeth. Today, he brushes three times a day. He brushes himself, but we set it up for him. He had to relearn all these daily living skills that people take for granted, from eating, to managing in the bathroom, to brushing teeth.

Eliya: You were the father of a typical child, a bright child, a social child. I assume that like every father you had expectations for him, and then suddenly he's a totally different child. What did this do to you?

Elazar: Because he's a very good-looking boy, and a very cute and adorable child, it would be very depressing to focus on my failed expectations. But we can choose what we focus on.

Instead, I focus on the reality that this was meant to be. I have to say I'm sure that it would be different if he was my only child, or if I had a smaller family—I don't mean to minimize the importance of every child, and the importance of every child as an individual world. But it does help that we have a family with his nine siblings, who are all very well-adjusted. Now five of them are married and with children, and it helps that all of us, including Dovid, are interactive in their lives as well.

We didn't have an issue of *coping.* We accepted that this is what G-d wants, so what's the best we can do for this child now? That's how we relate to it.

There have been hard moments. I went back to America for a bar mitzvah in one of the families in my synagogue. It's not easy to watch other boys who were his friends and are his age, reading the weekly Bible portions and making their speeches. I'm happy for them, but I say it's a blessing that my wife wasn't there to see all these people and the strides they have made. It would have been much more emotionally difficult for her.

Eliya: Was there anybody who gave you strength and support along the way, or did you just go it alone with your wife and family?

Elazar: In February of 2007, four months after the accident, my daughter got married. Actually, she started going out right before the accident, and the accident happened in the middle of their dating. I told her to continue, even though I hadn't met this prospective son-in-law because he was in Israel. I didn't want to hold it up, and they ended up getting engaged.

The wedding was in St. Louis because we were all there, although he had nobody because he's from South Africa. He, his parents, and two of his friends who came from yeshiva were the only ones who were there from his side, and it wasn't so simple for them to come all that way.

Several days later, I went with my second youngest son, who was still on crutches from the accident, to Israel for the wedding celebrations that were held there. Just the two of us made the trip.

While there, we went to see Rav Dovid Abuchatzera in Nahariya. It's nice to get a blessing from a great man, although I'm not one who runs after blessings. Rav Abuchatzera said that in the merit of the outreach work connecting with unaffiliated Jews, our Dovid would "return to himself." There are different ways of interpreting that, but we interpret it as "It's not over until it's over." We're looking forward to a complete recovery when Dovid "returns to himself."

Thank G-d, we've seen tremendous improvement over the last seven and a half years, light years more progress than what any doctor or therapist would have imagined. No one in their right mind would have predicted that kind of progress. If you would have seen the original brain scans, they gave a tremendously different picture than what he's doing now.

Eliya: What kind of progress do you see?

Elazar: He's reading and writing in English and Hebrew. He's eating by himself and singing, which were all the things they weren't sure he would be able to do. It's amazing, though he's far from normal.

Eliya: How so?

Elazar: His social skills are very compromised because he doesn't have the filters. He'll just say things out loud and not realize the social environment he's in. I can't bring him to synagogue because he'll just talk loud. If I tell him to be quiet, he understands it, and he'll say, "I'm so sorry." But then another second later, he'll start talking again. He doesn't have the control.

Eliya: What are you able to do for Dovid now?

Elazar: We're praying very hard now that he should come back fully. I say to myself that a lot of teenagers are crazy, so hopefully these things will kick in, as the brain continues to heal and develop new pathways. They say that the brain is in transition during these years from fourteen to twenty-two. We're hoping that all this praying, and the therapies, and the fish oil, the vitamins, exercise, massages, and whatever else we're doing will come into play.

Eliya: Describe your personal relationship with Dovid now.

Elazar: He's the only one at home, so we have a very fun relationship. We're always very excited when we see each other. I do push him very hard. For example, any time we see steps, he knows that I say, "Dovid, what do we call steps?" He looks at me and says "free therapy." For instance, if we'll be standing at the bottom of steep steps I make him go up and down them without holding on to anything. I get screamed at by people who think I'm torturing a handicapped child, but Dovid *can* go up and down the steps without holding on. Obviously, I tell him, "If I'm not there, you better hold on." And he never falls, even though I'm always bracing myself in case he slips so I'll be there to catch him. I make him do stairs because it's great for balance, mental alertness, and all the things he needs to develop. We take walks and I make him do stairs by himself because that's part of therapy.

I remember when he was at a children's hospital for therapy. They put a stool on the floor for him to step up and step down, and he couldn't do that. I remember when they put him on the steps of the hospital and told him to try and go with a side step, and he didn't know how to do that. Nowadays, he's up and down stairs and he never falls. If he does slip, he catches himself by the rail. He's very fast and alert.

Eliya: What are your particular challenges with Dovid now?

Elazar: He has a private tutor who has been with him for a year and a half. The tutor did phenomenal work with him: reading, translating, writing, and all sorts of puzzle-type things. Dovid can sit an hour and a half with the tutor and concentrate. I don't have the patience to sit and learn with him. I need to have others do it.

It's difficult when I take him to synagogue. I've made him do the prayer service by being really strict. I tell Dovid, "Stick your finger on the place and don't look up from the prayer book at all." Every time he'd look up, I'd say, "Put your face back in that book right now." I've had him do an entire evening service a few times, from the beginning to the end. But I do it by also giving him a lot of compliments. It's done with a *lot* of effort, and I don't do it regularly, but I push him to try to reach his potential.

When I take him to synagogue and he doesn't really make it through the beginning prayers or doesn't really even start, that's hard for me. I wish he'd be able to be there, because I know he can, but he doesn't always have the focus due to his attention deficit.

Plus, he's over-stimulated when he's around people. Dovid does well in a private setting, such as when he's with his tutor in a small room, one-on-one, or when he's the only one, without any noise and distraction. It's hard when he gets into a large crowd, as happens in the synagogue. He gets over-stimulated and starts talking in a high-pitched voice.

"Oh, Dovid," I say, "speak in a lower voice. Come on, low voice. Come on, lower, lower. You can do it." It can be hard when we're in public.

Eliya: What kind of challenges have there been between you and your wife?

Elazar: Not so many. I guess there are some small things, but nothing of major significance. For instance, she can't see him going up and down stairs. When I'm telling him to walk up or down stairs, she just gets nervous. She likes to stand behind and hold him, which I tell her is the worst thing for her to do: "It's not going to do any good to hold him from behind. If he falls, he's going to tumble down with you. If anything, stand in front of him."

We go through this all the time, because we're opposites. If I put a plate of food out for him, he's going to eat to the last drop because I'm standing there pushing him. When he says he's not hungry, my wife will give in. She has a softer approach.

When I put him to bed and close the door, I expect he's going to stay in bed and not get out. Most of the time he doesn't get up. When my wife puts him to bed, he can come out of the room four or five times.

These things can happen with regular children as well; it's not just a matter of a child with disabilities.

Eliya: Do you feel like you're a team?

Elazar: Definitely. As many tears as have been shed, more than can be counted, my wife and I have been blessed to be together sharing this experience. Not that there haven't been challenges; there certainly have, but we have faced all of them together. From the very beginning and all the way through, my wife has been a trooper. She "walks the talk."

Eliya: Does Dovid look to you for things that he doesn't ask for from his mother or anybody else?

Elazar: He might say, "Get me dressed," because it's hard for him. For instance, this morning I helped him put his shoes on. We have Velcro on the shoes to make it easier. I told him, "No, I'm not going to put them on. You put them on yourself."

He said, "I'm having a hard time. You can help me out a little bit, Abba, come on."

I said, "No." But I cheated a little bit and helped him by putting one leg over the other so he could put the shoe on the left foot.

He knows that if there's soda out—and he knows that I don't want him to have soda or something like that—or a piece of cake at a special occasion, he'll look across the table and say to somebody he just met, "Hi, could you please get me that piece of cake?"

They might answer, "Why don't you ask your father?"

And he'll say, "He's busy. Don't ask my father. Just if you could give me the cake."

He's very clever. I'll say, "Oh, Dovid, by the way, what are you asking him?"

He'll answer, "Don't worry, Abba, you're busy. Just don't worry about it."

I'll say, "Dovid, were you asking him for a piece of cake?"

"Yeah."

"Why don't you ask me?"

"Because you wouldn't give it to me!"

It's cute the way he's figured this out.

Eliya: When you look at Dovid and see that he's making progress, more progress than anyone would have thought possible, what do you attribute that to?

Elazar: We all would like to be on a higher level of faith and trust, but even if we're not there, we know it's true. So, when the doctors say that "he can't, he can't, he can't," I say, "G-d, You're running the world. You can, You can, You can."

I'm not going to be arrogant and say, "I've mastered the area of faith." In certain aspects, maybe I'm better than I think I am, but maybe I'm not. I can still keep asking, "G-d, make me wise enough to deal with this. You can do it."

What am I really asking for? It'll be a tremendous sanctification of G-d's name if Dovid turns out normal, because it defies nature and all logic. It shows that the only way this could have happened was not through the doctors, but through all the prayers from people around the world. "G-d, it will bring honor to Your Name, so give it to him. Let him come out to be a superstar."

Eliya: Did you seek support from any other Rabbis?

Elazar: Shortly after the accident I had a close friend ask Rabbi Chaim Kanievsky to add an extra name for Dovid to increase his chances of recovering. Rabbi Kanievsky suggested the name "Chaim," which means "life," but I already have a son named Chaim, so we changed his name to Rafael Dovid. "Rafael" means "G-d is the Healer."

A few days later I realized that I was having a hard time adjusting to his new name. "I'll do what I'm supposed to do, but, he's Dovid. I know he's Rafael Dovid now, but do I always have to call him that?"

When I asked the question, the answer came back from Rabbi Kanievsky: "Call him Dovid, but when he's honored in the synagogue at his bar mitzvah, and also on his marriage contract, it should say Rafael Dovid."

Eliya: How did you react when you heard this reference to Rafael Dovid's bar mitzvah?

Elazar: At that time, Dovid was in the Intensive Care Unit, and they were telling me it wasn't a day-by-day, but a minute-by-minute issue of his survival. I pulled out my Blackberry and looked at a calendar to see when he would turn thirteen and have his bar mitzvah. It turned out to fall on March 29, 2012. The neurosurgeons and all the assistants and nurses were watching me, and I said, "Everybody here is invited to Dovid's bar mitzvah, which is six years from now." They thought I was nuts, because they didn't think he'd make it another hour.

Eliya: You celebrated Dovid's bar mitzvah?

Elazar: Yes, he had his bar mitzvah. Obviously, it wasn't exactly typical because he had a hard time making it through the blessings without looking up and laughing and talking. It's very difficult that he's not focused and can't seem to do things from the beginning to the end without talking or making some kind of interruption. But, with all that and with G-d's help, he'll make it to his wedding as well, just as Rabbi Kanievsky said.

Eliya: Does Dovid talk of getting married?

Elazar: Listen to this. Yesterday I was walking up the stairs, and we were talking about a hat, because he had lost his skullcap on the way, so I gave him mine. He asked, "When can I have a hat?"

I said, "Dovid, I'll buy you a hat now, but you have to take care of it. I'm not going to buy you a hat for you to take it off and wreck it up. You don't have a hat yet for that reason. So, when do you want it?"

He answered, "I want a hat for my wedding."

I said, "Well, okay, but I'll even get you a hat now if you take care of your hat."

He said, "Well, I'd for sure like to have a hat for my wedding. I want to get married."

So I said, "Well, who do you want to marry?"

He said, "Someone gorgeous." At his age, he hasn't shown any signs of what might be normal for a fourteen-year-old, so this surprised me.

I said, "Well, how about a wonderful young woman who likes to teach Torah, someone like Mommy?"

Dovid said, "Yeah, that too, that too."

I thought maybe this conversation was a good sign that he's becoming normal.

Eliya: It certainly sounds like it. What do you imagine are the challenges ahead for you?

Elazar: As with any parents of a child with disabilities, I guess our challenge is what level of independence will our child have? Parents who have had Down syndrome children have a shocker from the birth on. We came into this when our child was seven, and we're still holding on to the hope that, somehow or another, his brain will dramatically continue to change.

I'm concerned about his ability to be independent, although I've never even discussed this concern with my wife. I wonder what parents do as they're getting older? Do they look to the child's siblings for help? We don't think along those lines, but that's a common issue in every family that has children with disabilities. This is about as much as I've ever discussed it out loud with anyone, just now during this last sixty seconds.

If you're asking me about the immediate challenges ahead, the main one now is to find a school that's most appropriate for Dovid. He's very smart, and we'd like him to mainstream as much as possible. It's just a matter of applying and bringing it all together.

The challenge is also to bring out the most without what the professionals call a "plateau" happening. We first heard the *p*-word at the six-month marker. Since then we don't ever say the *p*-word as in "plateau," only as in "progress." From the six-month marker we kept on pushing every bit of the way by doing vitamins, acupuncture, and all sorts of things. There wasn't anything we didn't do. The professionals didn't know where the successes were coming from. We know they were coming from prayer. Dovid should just continue to grow and improve.

Eliya: Are you getting the support you need from the various government agencies?

Elazar: No, it's taking too long. We've been going around in circles for about eight months trying to get Dovid occupational therapy in the rehab center of our health care provider. Our health care provider says it's the responsibility of the Department of Special Education which, in turn, says, "We're not going to do anything more." We appealed their decision but twice we have been denied. We now have a private occupational therapist come to the house for ongoing practice with daily life skills.

Dovid goes to the local sports center and has a personal trainer twice a week who gives him a good workout. This is so important for him. He needs more physical therapy to strengthen his arm and to work on his gait, stability, and walking without his left leg turning inward. He needs speech therapy to strengthen his cheek muscles so his drooling can be controlled. He also needs vision therapy. The list goes on. We are trying to do what we can.

Eliya: All the therapy must be very expensive?

Elazar: We have major expenses doing all we can for Dovid. We also supplement his daily learning at school with tutors. This we do on a private basis as it's not a service the school provides. At one point we had a learning partner/teacher come almost every night.

Eliya: Are you aware of what benefits are available to you?

Elazar: I'm not sure I'm aware of all the benefits that are available. We have a social worker who is supposed to keep us informed. There is assistance from the National Insurance, which helps, but it doesn't go very far in light of all of Dovid's disabilities. One benefit Dovid gets is fifteen days a year to attend camps or weekends organized for children with disabilities. This is an opportunity for him and a help for us as well. The transportation to school every day is also provided. This is also very helpful.

Eliya: Can you give us a picture of Dovid as he is now?

Elazar: He's a wonderful, happy fifteen-year-old. He goes to school but doesn't have a lot of friends. Kids his age don't really know how to relate to him because of his social style, which is compromised. But he understands. He enjoys reading books or having books read to him. He loves his iPad, which is his bar mitzvah gift from my mother. Somehow or another he knows how to work it, and he watches all kinds of things that amuse him. I suppose that's his escape. He continuously improves, and we continue to hope that he'll get there all the way.

Eliya: Thank you, Rabbi Grunberger.

5

MATT

Matt and his wife have five children—a fifteen-and-a-half-year-old girl, a fourteen-year-old boy, an eight-year-old girl, and twin boys less than a year. They didn't realize that their first son, Joel, had disabilities until he was a few months old and his development had not progressed as expected. Nearly fifteen years later, Matt still does not have a definite diagnosis of Joel's condition.

Eliya: Describe Joel to me.

Matt: Joel was born with very low muscle tone. He didn't walk until he was three. His muscle tone is still very low today. He's clumsy. His motor skills in general are not well developed. Fine motor skills are very difficult for him. For instance, he can't button his shirt. Physically, however, he is quite tall for his age. At first impression, Joel appears to many people as a typical fourteen-year-old. He is also on a very low cognitive level.

Eliya: Has Joel been given a diagnosis?

Matt: Nothing has been proven clinically or genetically. One neurologist claims Joel has Sotos syndrome, but that is just her theory. Sotos syndrome itself is not something with clearly defined levels of physical and mental abilities, so it is really hard to put a finger on what it is. But Joel has both physical and mental limitations.

Eliya: What were your expectations about being a father before you knew about Joel's disabilities?

Matt: I expected to have a normal relationship, whatever "normal" means. I looked forward to a relationship with him that would develop according to the norms at different stages in our lives. Certainly, I hoped it would be that way. Doesn't every father?

Eliya: How soon after Joel's birth were you aware that he had challenges?

Matt: After a few months, my wife saw that he wasn't progressing. He wasn't holding his head up, and his eyes weren't following where they should be following at his age. At our health fund's infant clinic, they told my wife not to worry about it, but she immediately started investigating.

We decided together that it wasn't something to push off and just wait and see. My wife was, and is, great in this way. She got totally involved in trying to get an appointment with this and that doctor, and trying to see what to do about this and that test.

We went to an eye specialist and for testing at a special center for child development.

Even though we got certain reports, we didn't get a specific concrete diagnosis or anything like that. Unlike Down syndrome or other conditions that have their own symptoms, it was very unclear in our situation.

Even when our child was not developing in certain areas, we didn't have a clear picture of what was going on and to what degree. After all the tests and examinations by different doctors, there was still a very big question mark.

Eliya: What did you do with Joel after receiving these reports?

Matt: From a very young age, Joel was in physical therapy three times a week, with a private physical therapist. We were putting a lot of energy into this, even though to a large degree we didn't really know what was going on. As far as going to doctors and giving him physical therapy, we were doing what we could to deal with the situation and try to improve it.

When he was a year and a half old, Joel was already going to a special kindergarten where he was one of the first students. We had a connection to the founder of the kindergarten through our family, so I think that helped us to get in.

Eliya: What kind of an experience was that for Joel and for you?

Matt: Joel didn't really know what was going on. For us, I remember that it was difficult. We had a special child and we didn't really know what his problem was and what to expect. He couldn't walk, he couldn't talk, and we were sending him off in a van every morning until 3:30 in the afternoon.

In the beginning, I remember it was so difficult, emotionally, for my wife to send off such a child that I took him to kindergarten myself, at least one way, if not both ways.

Eliya: Can you identify what those emotions were?

Matt: We were worried about Joel's safety, since he was a helpless child who couldn't walk or talk. We knew he was in good hands, but we were concerned that he was going away for so many hours at a time, especially in commercial transportation where the drivers are not always so friendly.

But eventually, after a few weeks' time, we realized that it was the right thing to let him go in the van.

Eliya: Did you have any kind of support from anybody at that time?

Matt: My in-laws were helpful in various ways. They have always been eager to help us any way they could. My mother-in-law was particularly helpful in identifying medical specialists. She also accompanied my wife and son to doctors' appointments, which freed me to maintain my schedule. That was a very big help.

I don't remember that I searched for support or help. I think it was just my wife and I handling things between the two of us.

Again, things were still cloudy, and we were not sure what Joel really needed. We did get some help from Joel's kindergarten during the three years he was there. His school generally deals with children who are more or less normal cognitively, but have physical issues. They provide a lot of physical and occupational therapy for the children. After three years, the cognitive issue was *the* primary issue. Therefore, we were advised to find somewhere else that was more fitting for Joel.

This time we had advice, but we were not ready to put any stamp of "retarded" on Joel, since he was still young and we didn't know what was going to develop. It was a very strong point during those years, when it was still unclear what would happen, that we didn't want to solidify things and stamp him with "abnormal child."

Eliya: Were you still hoping that he would turn out to be a typical kid?

Matt: Maybe not typical, because he didn't start walking and talking until he was three. However, some children do have late starts, and they can eventually make up gaps. We thought: *Who knows what could happen?* As it has turned out, the last thirteen years have been such an adventure that I can't remember conscious expectations of what Joel would become and then feelings of "Now this is not going to happen," or that type of thing. We were always trying just to plow forward to improve whatever we could, making whatever efforts we could to help Joel progress.

Eliya: As Joel developed, what became your challenges?

Matt: In the younger years there was the challenge to get him to stand for as long as he could by using special walkers to strengthen the muscles in his legs.

At the same time we talked to him a lot and tried to get him to respond verbally, so that he would start to speak.

As time went on, we began tackling the challenges of toilet training him and whatever he could do to gain independence—for example, putting a spoon in his mouth. Now he feeds himself.

He can't dress himself fully, but almost. He walks, and he runs a little. Verbally, he has slurred speech, but he can communicate and express himself to a large degree. Thank G-d, he walks and he talks.

We have a tremendous challenge getting him up in the morning and getting him out to the private bus that takes him to school. Medication that Joel takes at night makes it hard for him to wake up in the morning, and every day someone has to awaken him. He doesn't like to get up, which makes every morning a challenge.

Besides the fact that the earlier he gets to sleep, the easier it is to wake him, it helps if he has something to look forward to that day. Sometimes I give him something special to take to school, but that doesn't work on a daily basis.

When Joel isn't outside waiting for the bus and it leaves without him, I have to chase after it. I play cops and robbers at five to seven in the morning, trying to catch the bus driver before he leaves the neighborhood. That's one of my ongoing challenges.

Eliya: Have you been able to take pleasure from whatever accomplishments Joel has made?

Matt: Yes, we definitely took pleasure in them and were gratified. We have worked very hard to help him do whatever we feel that he's capable of doing. We know that the progress is gradual and things don't happen overnight. There were always surprises concerning if and when he would be able to do this or that. It's all question marks, and that's part of the adventure.

Eliya: Through all this training for Joel—the mobility training, the speech training, the self-help skill training, and so forth—were you involved in doing any of it with him?

Matt: Yes, my wife and I both had to, especially in the younger years. Of course, we had to take him to different places, and during the therapy sessions, we were asked to help since we provided another pair of hands. We also needed to observe the sessions so that we could implement some of the things at home.

Eliya: As you worked with Joel and saw how he was developing, did you see your role as a "father" change?

Matt: I guess I would describe myself as gradually finding my role as the father of a special child. It isn't something where you just say one day: "Here, this is my job, this is who I am." It was a gradual realization, but it must have been when Joel turned four or five that I realized this role was going to be for the long haul. Around that point, I understood: *This is it. This is what we have.*

Eliya: How did the presence of Joel in the family affect your daughters?

Father: Even as a small child, my older daughter was interactive with Joel. If she sensed that things were not the same with him, it took her a while until she could express the realization that her sibling wasn't a regular child.

I do have good memories of them together. Not that they don't interact now, but obviously it's different now.

My younger daughter is about five and a half years younger than Joel. For a number of years they were able to interact well together. That's passed already. In some ways she acts like a big sister and helps him with certain things.

Eliya: Did all the attention you gave to Joel impact in any way on how you related to your daughters?

Matt: We were spending a lot of time and energy with Joel, but we realized how very important it was that we should give our daughters as much time and attention as we could under the circumstances. There are times when you're a bit drained from dealing with a special child, and the other children take a backseat. You can't always give them the attention that they want and need, but we tried and we still try to take advantage of the time that we have together, especially when Joel is not around.

Eliya: It's common that choosing family activities revolves largely around the special child. Is that typical of you also?

Matt: Very much so. For example, as far as vacations or being invited to someone's house for a meal, almost nothing is to be taken for granted, and nothing is simple.

I'm describing things one hundred percent as they are, even now. In certain ways it's even more complex than it was before. We will not consider even a short vacation unless Joel is away, such as at a camp for children with disabilities.

Joel is a very emotional child and that's developed more as he's gotten older. Even though the physical challenges are less than they used to be, his behavior can be unstable at times because of his emotions. You get used to not knowing what to expect, but it limits you. If we want the family to go visit somebody, my daughters don't necessarily want to go with him.

As much as they love him as a brother, they usually don't even want to walk with him to the corner grocery because he may behave inappropriately. For example, Joel doesn't necessarily do it on purpose and choose to act out, but if he doesn't get something that he wants, it can turn into a tantrum.

Eliya: How do you relate to Joel and spend time with him?

Matt: It's hard to do many activities with him, because Joel is definitely ADD. I try doing things that he likes to do, such as playing with toy trucks, cars, and ambulances. I try to take him to synagogue once in a while, but I always have to hold my breath with that because I don't know how he's going to react, and believe me, things have happened.

He had a bar mitzvah ceremony and celebration in school. We had a lot of discussion about whether we would have something for him outside of school, and in the meantime, we haven't done anything. The bar mitzvah in school was so nice that we hesitated to try and do something else which might not be successful. We spent hours and hours and hours talking about it, but planning for all the contingencies is so complex that after all the discussion we decided to be satisfied with the bar mitzvah celebration at school.

Eliya: Tell me about Joel's bar mitzvah at school.

Matt: Due to his emotional instability and his ADD, it's hard to keep him focused on something for more than five minutes. In school, we're told that he can pay attention for longer periods of time, but not at home.

In preparation for the bar mitzvah, they worked very hard in school to help him say a blessing or something. He's not yet able to say a speech or explain something from the Bible. They videoed him in very short clips where he said a few words at a time, and they were able to show it at the bar mitzvah.

We were holding our breath at the bar mitzvah, but over the course of the two hours of the program, he held himself down and was in control of himself. He really came through.

We were on a high for something like a week after the bar mitzvah. We had so much joy from that, and it was such a good memory.

Eliya: Is Joel receptive to learning with you, be it text or how to do something?

Matt: He's not open to anything text-based. However, just recently we had a meeting in the school, and it was suggested that we should have certain fixed times to look at picture books with illustrations of certain religious observances which Joel is capable of doing. This would show him that he's older now and has more responsibilities.

Eliya: How does he respond to this activity?

Matt: What he wants more than anything else is attention. We haven't started yet with the picture books, but attention is what he wants above everything, especially from his parents. There's a good chance that he'll respond to having this extra time with me.

Eliya: What kind of social interaction does Joel have with people outside the family?

Matt: He goes to a group in the neighborhood with other children who have disabilities. A young man learning in yeshiva comes and picks him up, takes him out to this group activity for a few hours, and then brings him back. Joel returns happy and content.

Before this group started about half a year ago, if we didn't take Joel out, he didn't go out. And if he didn't go out, eventually he'd snap. This group activity has been a tremendous lifesaver for us.

Over the years, we've had teenage girls taking him out and bringing him to their houses for a certain amount of time, but he is too old now to spend time with teenage girls. So this new neighborhood program is a tremendous help.

Eliya: What do you project into the future for Joel?

Matt: The day-in and day-out challenges are so time- and-energy consuming that I told my wife we have to take things one day at a time, one week at a time. Joel is fourteen years old now, and this journey has been fraught with uncertainties and question marks all along the way. We're trying every day to make things better for him and better for us. Obviously, we'll have to think about the future more seriously, but we've been focusing on just getting through the day and not looking too much ahead.

Eliya: What keeps you going day by day, Matt?

Matt: What keeps me going day by day with him, when every day is such a challenge? I'm very grateful that I very much enjoy my daily routine of learning in the morning and teaching in yeshiva in the afternoon. That's more or less what keeps me going.

Eliya: What have you learned about yourself by virtue of having Joel in your life?

Matt: He's certainly taught me to be appreciative for what I have and to realize that life is about overcoming challenges, persevering, and hopefully strengthening my relationship with G-d.

If you would have told me fourteen or fifteen years ago that I would have a child like this, obviously I wouldn't know how to think about it or how to deal with such a situation. I'd be saying: "How could it be? And what's going to be?"

But now, as difficult and as challenging as it is, it's my life. I almost can't imagine how life would be without it—it's so much a part of me.

Eliya: Thank you, Matt, for talking with me about Joel, your family, and yourself.

6

DOV

Dov Chaitowitz and his wife, Linda, are the parents of Eliezer, a thirty-year-old with Down syndrome. Eliezer lives in an apartment with other young men with disabilities and is a vested civil servant in the Knesset, the Israeli parliament.

Eliya: Did you have any indication, Dov, before your son's birth that he would have disabilities?

Dov: Not at all. He didn't cry straight away when he was born until they gave him a slap. They took the baby away immediately without even giving him to my wife. Then the following morning, my wife called me at work and said, "Can you come over? The doctors want to talk to us." They didn't tell anything to my wife before I came.

We sat with them for half an hour and they told us Eliezer has Down syndrome. They said that there would be some testing, but there were clear signs.

Eliya: At the time of his birth, did you know anything about Down syndrome?

Dov: No, but they explained that all his development would be delayed.

One of the doctors told us that our son would not develop beyond the mental age of six. That prognosis was way off the mark. If you see him now, you would not believe it.

Eliya: Can you recall how you felt when you heard that?

Dov: That doctor's pronouncement put us off, but we tried not to take it too much to heart. Like any child, a child with disabilities has his or her own way of developing. I've always maintained that each child has to be educated according to his own way.

I remember my wife was all right when we were talking to the doctors, but when we left the room walking back towards the ward, she said that she didn't want the baby or to have any more contact with him.

I said to myself, and I remember this very, very clearly, that she would be the one to have to deal with him. She would be the one at home while I was at work. The big decision would be up to her and I would support it.

But that same afternoon when my wife nursed the baby for the first time, everything changed. I was the only one in the nursing section of Hadassah Hospital, and I remember it vividly. They brought our baby in and my wife took him and immediately began nursing him. I never heard another word about leaving him behind anywhere or giving him away for adoption, and I breathed a big sigh of relief.

During the next few days, the social worker placed before us three options. We could leave our son in the hospital, put him in an institution, or take him home. If we took him home now, we were told we could "try it a few years" to see what happens. I guess that meant we could give him away at some future time if we wanted.

We took him home.

Eliya: After Eliezer's birth, did you receive support from anyone?

Dov: Not really. We were assigned a social worker, but she was highly inefficient. She came once or twice, maybe. Then we were sent occupational therapists. When Eliezer saw one of them, no matter how small he was, when he saw her walk in the door, he cried and got very upset.

He started going to a child development center for children with disabilities. He was there for a couple of years, and then he attended a kindergarten which was not close. It was very difficult for my wife and me because Eliezer had to be pushed in a stroller and he was very heavy. Whenever I could, after my work I picked him up from school by taxi. Then Gan Harmony, a kindergarten program which integrates typical children and children with disabilities, opened up just across the road from us where we live in Jerusalem, and that was a real blessing for us.

Eliya: In the very early years, what emotional support did you receive?

Dov: Not much. Both sets of grandparents were very unhappy about the whole situation. My late mother-in-law was sort of waiting for a phone call that would come one day to hear that Eliezer had been cured. Also, my parents weren't supportive of the whole situation. We really did not have any parental support.

We received a few letters from friends of ours in London. My wife wrote to one of her very close friends, a rabbi, who sent back a very beautiful letter. He wrote that our special son was a present from G-d, Who gives these gifts only to families that can deal with the situation.

And my wife belonged to a very good support group for mothers which proved to be very helpful. But without parental support it was difficult for us in the early years.

Eliya: Would you say that you and your wife were able to work together as a team, or did one of you take more responsibility than the other when it came to providing for Eliezer?

Dov: We worked together. Occasionally, there were differences of opinion as to exactly what to do, but mostly we were together.

Eliya: How did you know what to do?

Dov: We didn't know. We had some guidance from the child development center and some from school counselors when Eliezer entered first grade. Thank G-d, Eliezer was never a difficult child. He's a very friendly child, and thank G-d, he's high functioning.

Learning to walk was a long and slow process. Though he was late to walk, the whole family was excited when he finally did. We tried to take everything in stride.

Then one day, we discovered that he could read. What do I mean "discovered"? One day my wife was sitting on the couch with him reading a story in Hebrew and Eliezer repeated a line that she had just read. And then he read the next line before she could read it to him. In kindergarten Eliezer began receiving instruction in reading, but we had never heard him reading on his own. Suddenly to us, he put all the words together and was reading. Relative to the other children, he was late in reading, but I felt very positive about his accomplishment.

We haven't had too many difficult times with him and we have learned his weaknesses. Eliezer doesn't have a high threshold of pain, for instance. Also, if there's a change in plans, most people can deal with it straight away, and they say, "Oh, so that's what's going to be." With him, if you know of a change, you have to tell him in advance: "There's a change in plans, and this is going to happen, and that's going to happen, and we're not going to do this, or we're not going to do that."

Essentially, he's a wonderful child, and we feel very blessed with him.

Eliya: Did Eliezer have medical problems at some point?

Dov: Yes. I don't know why, but when he was born, they didn't tell us anything. When he was about five weeks old, he was in the hospital because of cellulitis at the top of his leg, and while examining him, they found that he had a heart problem.

Following that discovery, he was under the supervision of a doctor at Hadassah Hospital for a year. The doctor wanted to operate to correct the problem, but he wanted Eliezer's weight to go up to ten kilos before doing so. So every couple of months, he was examined by the doctor.

After a year, the doctor discovered that the hole in Eliezer's heart had disappeared. There was no logical medical explanation for the discovery. The doctor lifted his hands and eyes heavenwards and exclaimed: "This is the only explanation."

It was suggested that we do an operation to reduce the size of Eliezer's tongue, but my wife and I had heard conflicting reports about this operation and its success rate. We felt that we didn't want to subject our son to the surgeon's knife unnecessarily, so we didn't do it. And in the course of time it hasn't been necessary. His tongue doesn't stick out and it doesn't impair his speech in any way.

Sometimes when he has a cold his speech is a bit unclear. But basically, his speech is quite good and it doesn't worry him.

Eliya: What did you do to help your other children accept their special brother?

Dov: At the time of Eliezer's birth, we explained the situation to the other two children and just took it from there. They were young, but I think they understood, because in later years and still now they each have a very close relationship with their siblings. So I don't think having a brother with Down syndrome affected their lives in any way.

I do remember, though, that occasionally they would get angry. They would say: "Why isn't Eliezer doing this, or that, and the other?" Or, "Why is he getting this or that?" But we tried as much as possible and were very careful that he did not get extra-special treatment. He was expected to do as much as he could do.

Eliya: How did you find an appropriate school for Eliezer?

Dov: As far as schooling, we were told, "Try Nitzanim, a special-education school in Jerusalem." So we called Nitzanim, and they said, "Yes, of course. Bring him for an interview." We did and he was accepted. And he was so happy there. From ages eleven to fourteen he had a male teacher, which was very helpful for him during those formative years.

His school experience was always very, very positive. He knew most of the children in the school, both ones older and younger than he. When we would walk him to school in the morning, children would say, "Eliezer, good morning... Eliezer, what's happening?" They all knew him, and he knew them all.

His teacher got married a week before Eliezer's bar mitzvah. We made a festive meal celebrating the bar mitzvah and at the same time his teacher's wedding. So as Eliezer was now a bar mitzvah and a fully entitled adult, he was eligible to recite one of the seven special blessings said at celebratory feasts held during the seven days following a wedding. Seeing Eliezer behaving as a full-fledged "adult" was very moving.

We have a lot of gratitude to Nitzanim, because their whole approach was very positive.

Eliya: I understand that Eliezer is an avid reader.

Dov: Oh yes. He loves reading. The first book he'll pick up is about the weekly Torah portion, and it doesn't matter if he's read it six times in six previous years. He loves Torah, and he'll read the writings of the Prophets. He remembers stories from the Torah that he's learned in school.

Eliezer's love of Torah makes me very happy. In fact, one time we were talking at the Sabbath table about that week's Torah portion, *Naso*, where the Haftorah [reading from the Prophets following the weekly Torah portion] is about Manoach's wife. She had a vision of an angel, and we were discussing it. Eliezer said, "Her name was Tzelafanid." That was a conversation stopper if there ever was one. He knew this detail and spoke it out at the appropriate moment.

When we went to check it, we found that he was right. Eliezer had learned this in school two or three years before graduating, and he had remembered it after all that time. Now we talk about it every year when it comes up.

He likes other books as well and enjoys reading about the comic strip character Tin Tin.

Eliya: How has your relationship changed with him over the years?

Dov: As with all my children, I played together with him and helped him during his childhood. We learned together, and after he started to read, we read all kinds of things together.

He doesn't live at home now. He's home only every second week for the Sabbath, and there's not really that much time, but we learn together and go to synagogue together. On Shabbos afternoon he also learns Torah with somebody in the neighborhood for a half to three-quarters of an hour.

If he doesn't meet with his learning partner, I will pick up a book and we'll go through it together. It's things he might know already, but it's nice just to sit and be with him. If there is time in the evening after Shabbos, we play together or do things together.

I enjoy spending time with him.

Eliya: Does your son relate differently with you than with your wife?

Dov: It could be, but I don't really notice it. If I'm not around, he'll sit with her. He relates to both of us in his own way by talking with us and telling us what's happened. Sometimes it takes time for him to tell us things he wants to tell us, but we don't have any trouble with that. He does communicate, but in his own way.

Eliya: It sounds as if whatever challenges you've had they were not difficult challenges.

Dov: No, they have not been difficult, but I have had challenges. When he got a letter from the army, I took him to the examination board. They saw him straight away and they said, "Here's your exemption," and that was that. Then he saw his brothers go in, and I had to explain to him that it was different for his brothers.

He also saw his brothers getting married, so he made a calculation of the difference in age between the first one to marry and the second one. He said to me one day: "Well, in two or two and a half years I'll be getting married." He had made that calculation. He's not very good at arithmetic, but he made that particular calculation.

Eliya: Does he still talk about getting married?

Dov: Yes, he does, but I don't encourage it. The marriage of young adults with disabilities is a whole other subject on its own. Somebody I know says to me every so often, "*Nu? Nu?* So when is Eliezer getting married?"

Eliezer is very happy where he is now, and I don't want to upset anything. He lives in a very good apartment with other kids, and he's got a wonderful job. I feel that he's at a stage now where he's happy in his life.

Besides, a marriage relationship between individuals with disabilities is not the same relationship as normal people have. Their living together would have to be constantly supervised, which isn't so easy to arrange or to maintain. I don't know if it's worthwhile upsetting what is working so well for him now, to tell you the truth.

Unless he met a young woman, somebody whom he really liked, somebody he got attached to. If it had to be, or somebody suggested someone, or whatever, one of my stipulations would be that it would have to be a girl with Down syndrome.

In Eliezer's apartment, all the boys are Down syndrome and from what I can see, these boys all get along so well together. I think that if Eliezer married a girl with another special need, it would be more difficult for him.

Eliya: I understand that Eliezer has been living away from home for five or six years now. Under whose auspices does he live?

Dov: Aleh Siach, an agency in Jerusalem which serves individuals with disabilities. I would like to mention the fact that we are extremely grateful to them, and to Rav Perkal in particular, for everything they've done.

In Eliezer's apartment they've placed boys with Down syndrome together, which means that they all know how to get along with each other and understand each other.

Eliezer has a few problems in the apartment, but that goes without saying. Any household has its ups and downs. However, I wouldn't want to change it.

Eliya: In general, how does Eliezer get along with others?

Dov: He's a very sociable and conversant young man. If somebody doesn't like him, he can sense it right away. He went to one particular job where the person in charge didn't like him, and Eliezer didn't want to work there anymore. He didn't like that feeling of not getting on with a person. But when they get on with him, he gets on with them.

It's the same at synagogue. One of the men said to Eliezer, "I would be happy if you help me collect the Bibles after we are finished with them." And he did. In fact, that's where he picked up his learning partner for Shabbos morning as well.

I've seen this in other boys with Down syndrome as well. We have friends whose son was in Eliezer's class—the boy was very, very friendly. He wasn't so high-functioning, but he was very friendly with a lot of people in the synagogue. When we went to our friends for Shabbos, we'd go to synagogue with this boy. I would see him go around and say, "Hello, how are you?" He'd be backslapping this one and chatting with the other one.

Eliya: Since leaving school Eliezer has been working. Has he had vocational training?

Dov: Yes. His training has all been "on the job." His jobs came through an organization which places individuals with disabilities. He has worked at both Hadassah hospitals and in a bakery. He wasn't so happy in the bakery.

Then about five years ago, we heard about a project that the then Speaker of the House in the Knesset, Dalia Itzik, had initiated. She wanted to put into action helping individuals with disabilities, so she created employment in the Knesset for fifteen people. Eliezer applied and he was accepted. Now that he has been working in the Knesset for several years, he is a full civil servant with all the attendant rights and privileges.

Eliya: What are Eliezer's responsibilities in the Knesset?

Dov: He delivers mail from the Israel Postal Service and the internal mail of the Knesset to various committees and different personalities. He's very, very friendly with Ruby Rivlin, who was a previous Speaker of the House and is now the President of Israel.

Six years ago we got a call from the supervisor of the apartment in which Eliezer lives that there is to be a big ceremony and Eliezer is being promoted to the status of temporary tenure. Then about a year and a half later, at another ceremony, he received permanent tenure. We went to the ceremony.

After the ceremony, Eliezer took us to the area where he works, and we saw a nameplate with the name "Eliezer Chaitowitz" on the door. We didn't know that he had his own office until that moment!

Eliezer used to work for somebody who was more closely in charge of him, but that man retired, While there's somebody who's officially in charge of him now, I think Eliezer is really the head of the department.

I no longer have the responsibility of supervising Eliezer's work activity; any issues related to his work are now the responsibility of the supervisor of Eliezer's apartment.

Eliya: How does it feel to have your son working as a full-fledged civil servant in the Knesset?

Dov: One time, my wife and I walked around the Knesset with Eliezer. Nobody knew who we were. He went into one room before us and we heard, "Eliezer, Eliezer." He was being treated with tremendous respect.

Originally, they told us it would take him quite a few months to get to know the layout of the Knesset. It took him maybe a few weeks. He fell into this job so smoothly. As it's written in *Ethics of the Fathers*, there's no person who doesn't have his time and doesn't have his place. This is a prime example of that principle. And we're very happy for him, and he's happy in himself.

Eliya: Do you have any further ambitions for him?

Dov: No. If he maintains what he's doing, I'd be very happy. If he's as happy in twenty years time as he is now, I'll be very happy.

Eliya: To what do you attribute Eliezer's success in finding his place?

Dov: Where he lives is an important part of it. We bided our time until we found the living situation that best fit Eliezer. The first apartment option offered to us would not have been good for several reasons. The atmosphere of the neighborhood was very different than the one in which Eliezer was raised. There was no synagogue nearby, and Eliezer has always been an enthusiastic synagogue-goer.

We contacted another agency and met with them. They were opening an apartment in a neighborhood that was more suitable for Eliezer. He moved in there but the mix of boys was not correct and he had problems getting along there.

Eliya: How did you deal with those problems?

Dov: We were very upset because Eliezer was upset. He used to come home and say that he wasn't happy there. This one did this and this one did that. It really wasn't for him. I've always maintained, and I told the teachers this as well, that Eliezer thrives on being given challenges. He's not the type to just ride along. He needs to get the extra stimulation, and this was not stimulating enough for him.

We spoke with the supervising agency and they moved Eliezer to another apartment, and it has worked out very well there.

Besides the right apartment placement, what also contributes to Eliezer's success in finding his place is to have a good work environment. Many job placements for individuals with disabilities are repetitive, assembly-line kinds of jobs. That kind of placement wouldn't work for Eliezer. And of course, the people who work alongside someone with disabilities have to be understanding and supportive. Thank G-d, Eliezer has found what works for him.

Eliya: At this point in time, it sounds like you don't have too much responsibility for him, since he's really caring for himself with the support of his apartment supervisor.

Dov: Yes, very much so. We're both very happy that he is where he is and doing what he's doing.

Eliya: You mentioned to me, Dov, that you have become a mentor to a father with a boy who has Down syndrome. Tell me about that.

Dov: I remember how it started. This lovely couple had a baby boy who was Down syndrome, and somehow they learned that I had a boy like theirs. Within the next couple of days, they called me, and I went to the baby's circumcision celebration. I established a relationship with the father, and he started consulting with me. It's now about fifteen years that we know each other.

What was I able to give to him? Both my wife and I try to encourage and advise them. Over the years, the father would ask me all sorts of things on the phone, or we'd meet on the bus and talk a few minutes. We encouraged this couple to send their son to the school Nitzanim, and the last I spoke with the father a few months ago, he was very, very happy with the school.

Eliya: Would it have helped you if you had had a mentor relationship with a father experienced with disabilities?

Dov: Definitely. But that is not how it worked out for me. But again, you see how everything in life works out for the best, exactly as it is meant to work out. For example, over thirty years ago, we first settled in a town near Tel Aviv. But I developed health problems and the doctor recommended moving to either Jerusalem, Arad, or Tzfat, where the climate was better for my health. We finally decided to move to Har Nof, a neighborhood in Jerusalem, where we have lived ever since.

Eliezer was born just before we moved into Har Nof.

If Eliezer had been born where we lived near Tel Aviv, it would have been another story altogether. We would not have traveled to Jerusalem for the proper facilities; it was just too far away. Eliezer would not have had his experiences at Gan Harmony, which opened across the street from where we lived in Har Nof. Who knows how things might have turned out with him if we didn't live in Jerusalem. As it was, everything fell into place. G-d helped us a lot, and for that we're obviously very grateful.

Eliya: What have you learned being the father of Eliezer?

Dov: One thing I learned and that I mentioned before has to do with not changing things on the spur of the moment. I've always told the children if we were planning to do something that I hope it will happen, but "I don't promise" and if it does happen it is "with G-d's help." I learned a long time ago that if things don't work out, you've got to explain it to the children.

I also learned that each child is to be brought up differently—I learned about that even before Eliezer was born. It was strengthened because of Eliezer, but I noticed with the first two boys that each one has his own way of doing things. You have to guide him, but you can't decide for your child.

Raising Eliezer has shown me that I cannot be surprised or disappointed when something turns out differently than I expected. Even though my first two boys have turned out pretty much as I expected, Eliezer hasn't. He continually surprises me with what he can do. So I try to be more flexible; I don't feel I have to make an issue about every single thing. If a child wants to do something, he'll do it, and learn the hard way.

Each child is going to do what he feels he wants to do or can do, and you just have to guide him the best way you can, while G-d helps with the rest.

Eliya: Thank you, Dov, for talking with me.

7

JOE

Two of Joe's children seriously challenged his authority in reaction to difficult family relations. Despite his pain, Joe worked on himself and the family dynamics. In the process Joe gained deep insights into his community, his family, his marriage, and himself.

Eliya: When did your first child's rebellion begin?

Joe: We were not sensitive enough to understand the early signs we saw. On one hand, we were denying the problem to a certain degree, and on the other hand, we thought that it would work itself out or go away. In hindsight, we saw in Jake positive "specialness," very much earlier than the signs of "specialness" which were not positive.

Eliya: Tell me a little about that positive specialness.

Joe: It was not a cause for concern, but my wife described it once as not *playfulness*, which is positive without any negative to it, but as a little too *play-ee*. It wasn't hyperactivity and nowhere near that threshold. It was almost like too much bounce, a little more than you were expecting. But it didn't cause any problems. School was still okay for that child.

At what age did we see "too much bounce"? It was at a very young age, at the age of four maybe. It's only in hindsight that we understand how "too much bounce" might have played itself out later. What I'm saying might sound crazy, but it was like having a kid and a half. Over the top.

Eliya: When did you recognize that there was something that you would call a problem?

Joe: I think it might have been somewhere between ten and twelve that Jake started to have problems in school.

Eliya: Up until that point, what was your personal relationship with Jake?

Joe: I was far from being a properly involved father. I had a lot of contact in the house, but I was doing my "young father" thing, which was completely uneducated. I spent some time with the child, but I was not involved in any way that might have been useful for what was going to happen later.

Eliya: Was that typical of how you related to your other children?

Joe: I didn't play any favorites, and I like this child. When at ten or twelve there started to be difficulties in school, did that change how I related to him? I was irritated at the beginning. As the child later accused my wife and me: "I thought you and Mommy cared more about what the people thought rather than how I was feeling." That was his later observation, although we had thought we were really paying attention to him and to what was going on.

But at the beginning of the beginning, when we were hoping it would kind of settle down, there was a certain degree of worrying about what other people thought. That is damagingly true, and it's the worst thing that the child could think—that you actually don't give a darn about him, and you're more concerned about your status, how things will look, et cetera, which is all just a bunch of junk.

I'm angry about it now that the opinions of other people had anything to do with what was going on. I'm the kind of person who always prided himself on not giving a darn about what the outside world thought. But that's what was, and it was tremendously damaging and devastating for the child, and for us. I cannot say it strongly enough. It translates to: "What did you really care about? You weren't paying attention to the child. You were paying attention to yourself." But as things got more out of hand and more in the open then we could begin to pay attention to what was really happening.

Eliya: What kind of behavior did you notice?

Joe: Jake was already starting to hang out with the wrong kinds of kids, and so forth and so on. In the beginning, we didn't even know about that, but he started doing things that weren't okay.

Eliya: Did you seek advice?

Joe: Yes, and the advice was useless. At that point, G-d had not yet sent us the correct messenger. But also the situation hadn't yet deteriorated into that extreme mode that it can slip into when you finally realize that something much more serious is going on. By age twelve, things got serious.

Eliya: How did you try to redirect Jake's behavior?

Joe: Like every parent, we tried to put a patch on it. We said, "Oh! He'll play drums. That'll be good." Or "He'll go to a karate class, or some other after-school activity." Something to divert the kid from spending time with the wrong people. I tried those things, but they were useless.

Eliya: Were you able to communicate with your son about the fact that his behavior was inappropriate?

Joe: You have to understand that during this process, which stretched out over a long period of time, communication was not where it needed to be. It's not so much that there was a barrier; there was just *non-communication*, not from the child's side and not from our side. Since mothers tend to have more communication with their children than do fathers, this non-communication affected my wife much more. She basically was carrying the burden of it until we got to the actual cracking point.

Eliya: During this time, what was your relationship with your wife like?

Joe: Not good. Here's a piece of kitchen table wisdom. It isn't the situation with the child which causes the difficulties in the relationship between the husband and wife. It's because the relationship between the husband and wife is x, y, and z that makes for fertile ground for a child to have problems.

A solid relationship between the husband and wife goes a long way at the get-go to help the situation already be better, and for everybody to handle it better, both on the parents' side and the child's side. Our challenge from Jake was just G-d revealing to us how "not happening" our marriage was. By the way, the wife is always more aware of that "non-happeningness" compared to the often "wanting-to-be-clueless" husband.

Eliya: You call yourself "clueless." What caused that?

Joe: What caused me to be clueless? Non-confrontation of the situation is a simplistic way of describing it. I didn't realize the degree to which my wife needed to have cohesiveness and on-the-same-pagedness, things that were glaringly missing in our marriage. She needed a partner, but I wasn't it.

Eliya: How were you able to improve the situation and develop more cohesiveness with your wife?

Joe: One of the things that went a long way towards helping me be able to do that better was the recognition of my perceptions of the situation by an outside expert, a therapist. The therapist could explain to my wife my perceptions, and then my wife began to feel like, "He might not be involved, but it's not as if he doesn't have an understanding which could be valuable here."

That gave me validation, which I very much needed, because I'm self-doubting enough that I didn't really think I had a way to handle this kind of thing, except through prayer. Prayer certainly helps, but it doesn't deal in a hands-on way with the emotional needs of your child and your partner, which is ultimately the key.

Everybody knows this rule: If the child feels parents aren't on the same page, he feels he's living in a universe of chaos. Remembering all of this is very hard for me because it's painful to think how out of sorts that situation was. I'm not talking about what was happening to the child, but how out of sorts I was as a human being. Of course, this understanding is all in hindsight.

But there *was* a recovery. I became more educated. I began to center myself, become more stable in the situation, and more able to do effective types of things.

Eliya: Describe how your "recovery" took place.

Joe: First of all, of course, it took reframing my perception of the whole situation. That's a process. It doesn't happen as a crack insight—"Wow-w-w! Hey, I got it! Now I'll just do this!" It comes with work. First of all, you work against your own habits, the lock-in of your own perceptions, and your own problems. Whatever you haven't got solved up to this point will work to your disadvantage.

Best thing is to get yourself all straightened out before you have any kids at all. That would be the best, no question. Everybody knows that. You want to walk into a situation with your children as a healthy parent and not one who all of a sudden needs correction at the same time. That's very ineffective and very, very disconcerting, because it's a lot of stuff to do at one time. Basically, it's like being in a fog. When you're uncomfortable in that kind of situation, avoidance is the easiest reaction.

Eliya: What allowed the fog to lift?

Joe: That's a giant question. It was a whole long process of talking with people who were expert about these situations and having them help us begin to do the work that we needed to do as a couple. And then we were able to begin to give proper help to Jake.

A marriage is really about being partners—beginning, middle, and end. Anything that's missing from that will not only cause the parents to be ineffective, it will cause them to be destructive—to each other, to the family, and to the child. This is basic Family 101.

But you only know it after you begin to pull it together.

Husbands are involved in their learning, in their career, whatever it might be, thinking that parenting is the wife's job; this thought is very destructive. But you should know something: Everybody, even with fathers who are way, way far ahead of where I was at that time, when the situation goes south, they're going to be asked to do things that they don't know how to do yet. They are called upon to do what they haven't yet done, as involved fathers as they already are.

This happens because G-d is going to tailor-make a situation that will push you over your line so you can grow from the challenge. It's not a matter of: "I took Family 101, 102, 1001…I'll give you credit for being there."

G-d has plans for you. It doesn't mean that a child will be all of a sudden problematic. Whatever it is, you're as prepared as you are now, but if your patterns of behavior need to be broken, G-d will break them.

Eliya: Jake is not your first child, is that correct?

Joe: No, he isn't. That's also an interesting thing. The family constellation makes a difference in who gets and gives what from and to whom among the siblings.

Jake was actually not in a bad position, being number four out of seven. Even though he's a middle child and you could automatically go into that over-simplification of middle-child business, it actually was good in a certain sense, being a middle child with the buffering he got. The child right above him took a very heavy hit from the oldest child, who was a parentalized child.

Eliya: What do you mean by "parentalized"?

Joe: "Parentalized" means that the oldest child was a parent stand-in in a number of situations. As the oldest child, they were capable of taking care of their younger siblings. However, that's not always good for the "parentalized" child or for the younger child. And it also means that things are not going to be handled exactly as they would be handled by the real parent.

The oldest child was "parenting" the third in the lineup, so Jake was not being bossed around. I don't think he had a particularly hard time from those above or below.

Eliya: What effect did Jake's behavior have on the family constellation?

Joe: It started to wreak havoc in ways that we were not even prepared to be prepared for. The child right below Jake was the good child but he, too, was also affected. He started to question himself, not in terms of the family norms. He had been sort of left in a vacuum because the problematic child sucked all the attention of the family; everybody starts to get really sidelined, whether they're above or below that child. That's a well-known syndrome.

Younger children wanted to emulate their older rebellious brother at a certain point in their careers. We had to really get involved there, but by that time, we were already in better shape to handle that part.

One particular younger child said something to the effect of: "I'm going to outdo Jake." And he was highly capable of doing just that.

Eliya: Did that mean you had two children at the same time who were having problems?

Joe: No, Jake was already well on the road to being all right and getting things together. This younger child had way more horrific things happen to him, starting from kindergarten. He suffered emotional abuse from a teacher. What happened branded him and scarred him very deeply. He remembers it perfectly to this day, even though he was only three and a half to four and a half years old at the time.

Eliya: What was it like for you to see your children pulled in different ways in reaction to Jake?

Joe: There's another syndrome, which is also famous, but I don't want to oversimplify the situation. The more awareness that G-d gave me, the more, of course, I felt guilty for having messed up earlier in my role as a father, and that kind of made me *inactive*, not *inoperative* and not *ineffectual*, but it kind of shut me down. What do you call that when you can't make a move, when you get paralyzed?

Eliya: Stymied.

Joe: Yes, stymied. I was taking responsibility and owning it, but I didn't want to do anything about it. I felt bad about it, and that ended up being a stupid excuse for not saying, "Okay, this is what I did or didn't do in the past, but *now* what am I going to do?" And then I let the situation deteriorate even more.

Obviously, I don't feel proud about that at all.

You just have to know that everybody gets stymied here. That's what you're going to do, and even though I believe in the principle of "Don't let your guilt get in your way," that doesn't mean I'm not going to let my guilt get in my way, because I will, most probably.

Eliya: How did Jake's situation turn around?

Joe: The situation spun so far out of shape that it was already at the extreme. The police got involved because of certain incidents. Jake went to rehab, which failed three times. It was not yet the time for the right solution from G-d.

The rehab facility finally did it, even though Jake had run away from there also. We were already getting in better shape at that point. We had to come every other week, together with Jake, for family therapy. We also came for therapy with our other children every once in a while. The therapist was extremely effective. The counseling helped us to heal and helped Jake to properly use his rehab situation.

Jake succeeded from that point on in terms of building healthy relationships and the other stuff that goes with it. He was in a halfway house at a certain point, he got a job, things became okay, and he got clean from addictive substances.

Eliya: Did Jake also return to your religious values and practices?

Joe: When he rediscovers the religion part, he'll rediscover it, but the important thing is that there's a healthy human being there now.

Eliya: You have a rather high-profile public position, Joe. Did this experience affect your position in any way?

Joe: Nobody knew about it except for the people in the neighborhood who saw Jake, so my job was not affected, nor was my wife's. I'm not in an environment like that. I do my job, I'm valuable where I work, so even if it was known, that wouldn't have broken it. There was already a phenomenon happening in the world of "Even in the best families…" But when we first started, it wasn't in the best families. I'm not claiming I'm a "best family," I'm just saying that when the situation with our child became known it was never a threat to our social standing.

Eliya: How did your extended family relate to the situation?

Joe: Jake always showed up properly for family events, weddings, and stuff like that, so the family could not make an issue out of it. Besides my immediate family certain people within the family knew, but basically, the family at large did not know.

Eliya: Was the experience in any way a challenge to your religious outlook?

Joe: Just the opposite. It made me realize how much I was not where I should be, spiritually. You could be as religious as you want, you could have impeccable character traits, and things are still going to happen.

I was willing to own that part—that my practice of what I believed should have been somewhere else also. But I was definitely in great contact with G-d, especially as things continued to go on. What was important was having that contact and then going to another level; getting broken and then being more real and not pretending.

Eliya: You feel that you had to be broken in order to grow the way you did?

Joe: Absolutely. Only in hindsight, but yes, absolutely.

Eliya: Can you describe what broke you?

Joe: The situation was not in my control, at all. I'm not even a control freak, but I realized *I don't have the tools to handle this yet.*

Eliya: At what point did you feel "broken"?

Joe: When things were at the extreme. When they hit bottom, in our relationship with Jake and with the situation itself. It kept happening time after time. We thought, *Oh, it can't get any worse than this,* and then it *did.*

Eliya: Was there a particular incident that occurred, and after that incident you felt broken?

Joe: Let's not look at it as the extreme kind of breaking point, but it was just another push and another push and another push.

Let me add in something very quickly here. During that time, my wife started to travel out of the country to take care of her mother. I was the only parent at home for the first part of the therapy with Jake. Suddenly, the responsibility and the involvement lay squarely with me, which I accepted gladly. I was not only feeling no resentment, but I was even happy about the opportunity.

My wife and I began to realize from our therapy that my wife was taking tremendous responsibility and leaving me no room to take responsibility. This was one of the insights we got only later in the process, and that was very healing because now I *had* to be involved, and I didn't do it only by default. That's when I started to have an incredibly deep relationship with Jake. And it has continued and only gotten greater, and deeper, and better. I have a relationship with Jake that nobody else in the family has.

Eliya: You got to be his father.

Joe: Yeah, but completely! Jake had said, "You weren't there for me," at a certain point. I couldn't have given him the protection he was looking for because we weren't even aware of what Jake was getting exposed to. As far as a child sees it, especially when it comes to that kind of child, the father is supposed to protect, no matter what the extenuating circumstances. Yes, that's correct, I got to be his father.

Eliya: How did your new awareness and experience of being a father to Jake impact on your relationships with your other children?

Joe: I was very playful with my children when they were younger, by the way. It's not as if I never talked to my children. I used to read them stories at night, stuff like that. I actually enjoy young children. I like the way they think and the way they don't think. A part of me is still a kid, so I liked that. It was just great for us.

But I'm just saying that when they start to hit the harder ages, all of a sudden, you get thrown into an adult position, and you can't be with them in that way. I don't say I was a pal to my kids, but I'm just saying you can't be that teddy-bear type of father, not that I am exactly.

Of course, it spilled over no matter what, because I was already feeling better and more successful about myself. The change in me had good effects on everybody. But unless you take the relationships kid by kid, and repair what needs to be repaired, and deepen and further what needs to be deepened and furthered, then it's not going to all of a sudden get better automatically. Nothing automatically happens with children. It all has to be worked on.

Eliya: As you were working to rebuild your relationships with your children, what was happening to your relationship with your wife?

Joe: My wife will testify now that we have worked *our* relationship to a place where it's what it always should have been. And she can live with it. When I say "she can live with it," it means that it's what it's supposed to be.

She's a very happy woman right now, I'm proud to say. And she's proud of me for making her feel like that. Knowing she feels that way helps me to be better all the time. I can even help my father be a better father to me, and my father is already much older, and I'm a much older son.

Eliya: Can you elaborate on how becoming the father to your children that you wanted to be has changed how you are a child with your parents?

Joe: You have to understand that I'm sixty-four years old now. Once you start *to get the point*, you can use all your other situations to begin to see the other person's point of view. It's invaluable.

I was always more or less the sensitive type. I'm the oldest son of my family. I was always sensitive to my parents, because the oldest child usually is. But then to be able to see that what my children needed from me is what my parents need from me, I was able to behave with my parents way better. It's a very big plus, and I'm feeling quite successful now. I'm not bragging—I'm just saying that it's a good feeling.

Thank G-d, my parents are still alive, so I can do it with them. They should be well and live to be a hundred and twenty.

Eliya: How did your parents react to their grandchild's situation?

Joe: That was a little tough. They didn't like to hear that there was a problem with Jake, so we didn't want to burden them with it. That's the kind of relationship I have with my father. He's not the kind of father that steps in and helps you take care of something.

He tried once by giving a heartfelt lecture to all the kids. He thought he'd snap Jake right back into place, but what my father said didn't speak to Jake. It's a different generation, and it doesn't work like that. My father had no idea what Jake was into, and that was before his situation had gotten to the extreme.

I was moved by what my father said, but that wasn't it. First of all, the grandfather is not the father.

My wife and I made the decision not to burden our parents too much with our problem. When it came to my parents, I was still the child. I got empathy from them, and that was good for me. I needed a little bit of that, but I didn't go into details. It was not useful, and I didn't want to bias them against Jake.

I have no right to disclose what's private. My child is not their child, directly. My child has a right to struggle and grow, and everybody doesn't have to know all his private details.

Eliya: As you went through a process of developing awareness of yourself and others, what changes took place in you?

Joe: The change in me that was in process with Jake was really thinking about what it would take to speak to that child's insides. And I started to succeed very well. I had been able to do it before this whole crisis, but the point was that I wasn't *doing it* with him.

I began to think about how I could communicate with Jake so that he could hear me. I was able to do this with non-family people, easily, because that's exactly what I do best. I'm not bragging, I'm just telling you.

Jake began to realize that I had some valuable insights, and I started to get positive feedback. My wife was able to say to me: "The way you spoke to Jake was brilliant, wonderful."

The interesting insight here is that exactly at the place where you want to be doing the thing more, you're all gummed up. The trick is: Even if you know how to do this, you must be able to do it *then*, when you need to do it. That's very hard. When it's that close, when you are right in it, it gets much harder to be your best.

Eliya: How did you use what you learned with Jake when you went on to focus on the second child who challenged you?

Joe: We applied to Rami everything we had learned from Jake. Because of very many factors, the situations are very different. Some of these factors are external events that continue to make Rami's situation different. From our psychological point of view, the situation is handleable, and we are succeeding.

Rami is benefiting from our experience, even if we're not going to solve it the same way. We're flexible as we use the tools we've gained. There's also stuff that is completely, but completely, beyond our control.

Eliya: How is that for you?

Joe: We're not falling apart, even a little bit. It pains us, but we know our limitations. We are happy people, but pained by the pain of our child. It's completely different than it was with Jake.

I want to say proudly that we did grow through it all. We're not Olympic champions, but I'm telling you, we grew. This works and Rami knows that it works, because he sees how good we are with him.

He also knows that it's not only about us—not that I'm looking to get out of owning it or having responsibility, but I'm saying that everybody's doing the best they can. Rami is also very conscious and self-aware, and he knows very well what's going on.

One of the big mistakes that I made was that because I'm a well-read and worldly person, I thought I had seen and known about very many things. My challenges with the children were there to teach me that even with all that experience and knowledge, I was still going to have to grow into a solution.

That was absolutely true, and it was true even with Rami, when I couldn't just walk in with the knowledge I had gained from Jake. There was always going to be something different because you're never able to be completely inside the other person. You don't know how it feels to be them, no matter how sensitive you are. The breakdown that Rami went through has been a *whole* different experience than what his brother went through. I can't even begin to describe Rami's situation.

But I'm not bad at this game. I get it, and Rami knows that, and he knows that I *get* him. That has been the basis of our talks, and Rami recognizes it when he says, "Daddy gets me." He knows he can say things to me and I really get it.

This has at least held the situation to what it is at this point, and that's good. I feel successful even with just that.

Eliya: You have had a deep experience developing as a father. Now that your children are grown and out of the house, what is fathering like for you?

Joe: I'll take for example one of my other children, who is successful and had just a little bit of a bump in school at a certain point. He's a got a wife and children and is a wonderful, fine person.

I have a lot to work out with him, and I see it's not over. We just had an hour-long discussion the other day. This is going to sound funny, but it was a disagreement about how to look at a certain religious teaching. Underneath the surface, it had to do with our psychological outlooks and his resentments which he still harbors.

I know that because he has a negative view of how he explains the particular teaching, and I have a very, very positive view. I always have had a positive view, but the point is that he didn't get the benefit of inheriting it from me. He didn't get it because of how I did or didn't treat him. I realize that he needs that positive perspective from me.

I have years of work there. He's married and out of the house already, and he goes to somebody for counseling. He's got some of his own issues to work on, but in the end, it's going to have to be between him and me, because I know that it needs to get done.

We have to be fathers all our lives. The best thing you can do is to be the kind of father who, even if you're not in this world anymore, is sitting on your child's shoulder in a good way. You want to be a positive asset for your family that they can access even when you're gone. Leaving a legacy entails exactly that.

Have the big picture in your mind. This can be your strategy for not getting overwhelmed by your local situation. What would it take to be something that you would be proud of being, so that even when you're not around them, you'll be there? That's a wonderful way to help you guide your actions and decide how you want to exhibit your feelings, and what feelings to have and not have. And also how to be in control of yourself. You want to be a resource for your kids forever.

You do it as fast and as slow as you do it, but you must do it. It's not going to happen by chance. G-d wants us to act, decide, make decisions. Nothing's going to change without that. You have to decide to be different. You don't even know what different looks like yet. The first decision, before *what* to do, is that you're going to *do* it. Or, in certain cases, you're going to *stop* doing something. That's invaluable.

Children want to be reassured that you are actually a decision-maker. These are famous words; I'm not the first to say them. Children will push you to the limit because they want you to be in charge. It's not just about discovering limits, as it's often described in child psychology. Children want to get that parent inside of you going and saying, "I'm here." It's important, because then they can feel and say, "Good! I got a wall I can fall back on here. That's what I want." Who doesn't want that?

In the end you want to fall back into G-d's arms. If you don't think G-d is solidly behind you then you won't be able to catch somebody else. As always, I'm talking to myself. Whatever's missing going in one direction is missing from the other direction as well. That's exactly what's necessary for you to feel—that G-d is solid for you and you can always fall back on Him, because ultimately that is who you do fall back on..

You may also need a little bit of professional help or an outside opinion. But getting outside help does not mean dispensing with your responsibility. It is about learning that you can say, "Hey, I know what my kid needs. He needs somebody who is ready to catch him if he begins to fall." That's a great educator. You may not even know what you're talking about yet, but getting outside advice will help you easily figure it out.

Your child may not know how to express how he feels about being with you or getting support from you, but you'll know what it's going to feel like to have it. You will be able to say to your child: "Well, we had quality time tonight, didn't we?" And your child will be able to answer: "That's exactly what it felt like. Thanks, Dad, for the quality time."

And you will be able to say to him: "I like being with you."

Rami likes hanging out with me. We don't even have to say anything. It's the good presence we create that works. *Presence*, as in *being present.* I liked having that experience with Rami, and I liked hearing from him that he actually felt it too.

Eliya: Thank you for opening up so completely to me.

8

ALAN

Alan is the father of a handsome little boy, named Sammy, who didn't start speaking until he was about three years old. Professionals couldn't determine why and began tagging Sammy with a variety of labels. Alan never bought into any of the labels. Instead he worked to build Sammy without concern for the limitations which labels impose.

Eliya: Sammy is your second child. Was there anything prior to his birth that indicated he would have disabilities?

Alan: No. And not after his birth either. Everything was completely normal. Sammy was a normal baby. Happy in everything and seemed to be developing just fine, until he was around one year old. At that age babies usually start to talk. We kept waiting for his first words but they just weren't coming.

That's where it all started. It started with speech and for a long time it looked like Sammy had a speech problem. We took him for speech therapy to our health fund's well-baby clinic. But it didn't help. He didn't magically start talking.

At eighteen months he still wasn't talking. We consulted with a child development center, but they always give a speech issue more time before making a diagnosis to make sure there's actually a problem and not just that the child is a late talker. Not talking at eighteen months was still considered normal, so we continued to wait.

We only started at the child development center when Sammy was two years old. But after nearly a year at the center he still did not make much progress in speaking. Given that Sammy was only beginning to say words when he was nearly three years old it became clear to us that Sammy would need a special education kindergarten setting.

Eliya: How did you react to your son being so delayed in beginning to speak?

Alan: I wasn't very concerned about it. I didn't really think about it as a problem. In all that time we were just waiting, thinking that Sammy was just a "late" talker.

I spoke to my parents, who said that other kids in my family were also late talkers. So, I thought to just wait it out.

Eliya: Did you have expectations for your son? Dreams for your son?

Alan: I'm not the kind of person who dreams "I'm going to take my son and play baseball with him," or anything like that. I'm one of six boys, so having a boy was not a big deal. Having a girl was a much bigger deal.

Somehow even though Sammy has needed a lot of attention I managed to keep a positive attitude on things. I think that life has a way of distracting you at times. Like, you're excited about something and then a problem pops up, so it's going to make you forget about that excitement for a little bit and focus on the problem. That's how I feel. So I never really felt like my dreams were being crushed or anything like that.

Eliya: How was your wife handling this?

Alan: Her reaction was very similar to my mine. In the beginning she wasn't too concerned. But then later on, when it became clear that Sammy should be talking already, that there was a problem, so obviously we got concerned about it. That's why we went to see doctors and why we sent him to a special education kindergarten. My wife handled it very well. She was very caring, very concerned. Every step of the way was very thought out.

Eliya: What did the professionals have to say about Sammy?

Alan: Because of the communication problem the professionals have been concerned that Sammy is PDD (pervasive developmental disorder; on the autism spectrum). They have insisted on conducting all kinds of tests. Even though it's very, very clear to us that Sammy's not autistic in any way, even mildly, we have done the tests. All the tests that came back have said there's no indication of PDD.

My experience with professionals is that they like to label. They need it. A kid can't just *be*. My wife and I always fought against these labels. Just let him be who he is. He has his problems. But they *have to* have a label. They have to have a diagnosis with a label because without it they don't know how to treat. So they have an obsession with labeling.

Sammy's first label was dyspraxia (developmental coordination disorder or clumsy child syndrome). That label went with him to his first formal school setting, a special kindergarten for children with physical disabilities and speech disorders. He acquired a few others once he entered the formal school system.

Eliya: What challenges did you have to find a special education kindergarten setting for Sammy?

Alan: Well, there weren't such big question marks then as to what the issue was. It seemed like it was mainly the speech. But people were saying there were other issues. We initially thought that a proper program for him would be in a kindergarten which specializes in developing language skills. We found such a setting but as it turned out it was too advanced for him. It was for children who could speak but have difficulties with speaking, but not for children who have a total lack of speech.

Eliya: Can you describe what that means: "total lack of speech"?

Alan: Sammy was not able to express himself verbally at all. He made sounds. There was one specific sound that I remember the most, when he'd get very frustrated. It expressed very well that he was feeling frustrated. Yet somehow he was expressive. He was able to get what he needed from us, but the lack of speech eventually made it very frustrating for him and for us.

Eliya: What was his behavior like?

Alan: His behavior was pretty normal, except that he was extremely hyper, already between the ages of one to three. It expressed itself like an energy bomb: constantly running around, wild, out of control. He didn't have any physical motor problems. Not at all. In fact, he was very advanced. He was walking at ten months. Going out with him was incredibly stressful because you'd never know what he was going to do, how he was going to act up. It was very difficult to take him anywhere; we had to make special arrangements for someone to watch him every time we had to go out to run errands.

It was difficult, stressful. We couldn't go to a family gathering because he would just be too much. If we did go we just accepted that one of us was going to have to be with Sammy every minute. He had to be watched like a hawk because he could get into dangerous situations. When we'd walk in the street you'd have to hold his hand tightly because you didn't know when he might bolt and run onto the road. When he was awake, the whole focus was on him. He was extremely demanding.

Today, it's not as extreme, because he knows more now. He's wiser. He knows he can't run into the street. So it's not as stressful to go out with him. But still, there's a certain amount of logical reasoning that he doesn't yet have. And so he still needs to be watched very closely.

Eliya: What were Sammy's experiences in a group setting?

Alan: Before going to the special-ed kindergarten Sammy was in a regular day care setting. Was the day care able to provide for his needs properly? Maybe in the first year it was okay. He was very young still and didn't make unusual demands. It was just babysitting.

But then, as they started to do more things in groups, Sammy didn't really participate. He became very miserable at some point. All he did all day was ask for us and sit at the window by himself. When there was a group activity, he would go off by himself and play on the slide or something like that. Naturally, being that the setting was a regular day care, they just let him do it.

At the end of the second year there was a party where the children did things together for the parents to see. Sammy didn't want to take part in it at all. He was outside on the slide the whole time. I was sitting there, thinking, "What am I doing here?" It was then that I realized what his year had been like. I wasn't happy about it at all. I felt bad that he wasn't somewhere that was more than just babysitting. We saw at home that he really wasn't happy in the day-care setting. Toward the end of the year, when a kid is usually well used to going every day to his group, he would cry a lot in the morning before going. It's not normal for a kid to cry like that at the end of the year.

It was difficult to handle that. Did I seek help for myself? No. I didn't feel the need for it. We managed it somehow. It was difficult, but we knew that next year he was going to a program geared to children with special needs and it kept our hopes up.

Eliya: How did you react to putting your son in a special education kindergarten?

Alan: The program was for kids with motor and speech problems. Given Sammy's speech delay, I thought it would be good for him and it wasn't difficult to get him in. But when I first saw the kids in the program I automatically freaked out because there were kids with walkers, kids with all kinds of visual abnormalities and things like that. It was difficult because my son looks normal. If you would see Sammy on the street, he looks completely normal. At first I couldn't understand why they put my son in the same category as these kids who looked like they had horrible problems: they can't walk, they are always drooling, or have weird eye movements.

I didn't have any experience with kids who had these kinds of problems and I didn't understand what any of it meant. It just looked to me like "kids with big problems." So that took me a while to get over. But eventually I accepted it. It helped a little bit that there were other kids in the program who looked normal, who just had speech problems and things like that.

Eliya: How did Sammy react to his new school setting?

Alan: For him, it was just going to school. He moved into it with the normal reactions that kids have when they move to a new program. He cried a little bit, but despite that he was happy. Not like the year before, when he was still in the day care and unhappy.

He was actually doing things, learning things, and learning how to talk. The school offered speech therapy, occupational therapy, a lot of one-on-one with the speech. We already knew what to do at home with him. The school did not give us a program to follow, but at that point we already knew there was a speech problem, so it wasn't just "Can you say cup, can you say water?" We knew already not to do that.

We talked to him all the time because we knew he understood. We got to learn how much he actually understood of what we were saying and we more or less kept it at that level. And he eventually started to say words. In the first year of the kindergarten Sammy progressed from just saying words in isolation to making simple sentences.

Eliya: When you looked at your son, Alan, what did you see? A "special" child, or was he just your child?

Alan: I saw a "special" child. He was three and he wasn't talking. He would go to the park and he couldn't talk to other kids. Our friends were aware that there was a problem. They were supportive, understanding. But there were times, I remember, when we had to explain to other parents that "he just doesn't talk."

I remember one time Sammy got into a little fight with a kid in the park, and the kid's mother somehow got involved. I was standing off to the side and watching the whole thing. She was trying to get Sammy to apologize. He could get a little aggressive. He would push a kid off a slide or something like that. I didn't go there immediately to say, "Oh, don't bother. He doesn't talk." When he wouldn't apologize I think she got annoyed. She probably thought: "What a brat; he's just ignoring me." I finally went over and said, "I'm sorry, but he doesn't talk." It was a little strange, but it wasn't hard for me. It wasn't embarrassing.

Eliya: How would you describe Sammy's speech development in the kindergarten?

Alan: There seemed to be a very specific pattern in his speech development. He would acquire some language and be very happy about it because he could express himself better. I'd notice a huge jump in his speech. Like all of a sudden he's saying all these words he didn't know and doing so great. And his behavior would immediately improve. But as he got older his feelings became more complex and harder to express. I would see a regression in his behavior. I knew that it was because he was feeling things which he couldn't express.

There was a cycle like that. He would acquire a lot of language all at once, and things would be okay, and then a regression in his behavior and then he would acquire more language and things would be okay. There was a lot of up and down. It took me a while to recognize the pattern.

Eliya: What were you able to do for Sammy when you saw him frustrated?

Alan: There really wasn't much we could do with that frustration. We tried to figure out what was in his head. But a lot of times we just had to wait it out.

It was difficult for me to see my son frustrated, not able to express himself. It was very difficult. With his kindergarten also, they always wanted him to advance more and more, and my attitude was "Leave him alone, he's talking. What do you want?" Later on, I understood that there are other things besides the speech that he needed to get good at. I didn't get too upset about it. I thought, "Whatever it is, it'll work itself out. It'll be resolved."

Obviously it's hard to see your child frustrated. There was always the thought, "Oh no, he's not going to talk!" But then he would make a jump. It was so exciting for us. It was like, "Oh man, he's talking!" For like a year I couldn't believe that he was talking. But then he'd regress.

Eliya: Have you actively sought information to understand Sammy's particular problems and behavior?

Alan: Yes. Always. At one point, all of a sudden Sammy had these facial tics. It was strange. Then he had this vocal tic. So I immediately went online and I started looking. I got really worried that he might have Tourette's (an inherited neuropsychiatric disorder characterized by physical and vocal tics.) But the tics disappeared within two weeks. Occasionally I still see them, but he doesn't have Tourette's.

Has it been helpful searching for information online? Yes and no. Going online and researching symptoms is good for general knowledge, but it's also not good because it's always pointing in the direction of bad things, like Tourette's. From my online searching I was convinced that he had Tourette's because he had a facial tic and a vocal tic. But then later on when I spoke to a neurologist, I learned that Tourette's involves a lot more than just tics. It has to be for a certain length of time, which, of course, never happened.

Eliya: How has Sammy progressed in his development of social relations?

Alan: It has been difficult because there was always a gap between his speech and that of his peers. There was an issue in kindergarten where it seemed that he recognized his physical superiority over the other kids, since many of them had physical disabilities. The teachers described it that Sammy started to treat kids as objects. If he was on the slide, he'd just push the kid. It wasn't because he was a bully. He just got used to being the strongest and the most advanced physically. But that was a little difficult for me to hear, that my son is being aggressive and violent, because I'm exactly the opposite.

Eliya: What was the difficulty of saying "He's that way and I'm not?"

Alan: Your kid's behavior is like a reflection of you. As a kid I never liked someone who was a bully. I know my son is not a bully. It was difficult for me to hear this about my son, especially since it's not the way I taught him.

Eliya: You mentioned earlier about the professionals needing labels. Is labeling your son a "bully" part of that same syndrome?

Alan: The staff never really labeled him in a negative way. They didn't call him a bully. But I felt that other people were seeing him as a bully.

One afternoon at the school, a mother came to pick her daughter and exactly then Sammy hit the girl, and the mother got very upset. "He's a violent child," she told the teachers. When what the mother said came back to me, it was difficult for me to hear. He's not a violent child. He just doesn't modulate his emotions very well. He's prone to act out like that. Eventually the girl and my son became very good friends and later on I spoke to the mother and she was really okay.

Eliya: So Sammy has improved in his social relationships?

Alan: Yes. The kindergarten provided a behavioral specialist whom we met with every week. Gradually Sammy's social behavior improved but other problems developed. Starting in the third year, the structure of the program in the kindergarten changed. Sammy did not react well to the changes. There was a new teacher and different patterns of behavior expected of the children.

A couple of months into the new structure, it was clear to everyone that Sammy wasn't getting anything out of it. So we decided to keep Sammy at home. This was a decision my wife and I took on our own; it wasn't an arrangement worked out with the kindergarten; we just didn't send him to school. Later on we made it official that we were taking him out.

My wife had been talking about it early in the school year when we saw that Sammy began drooling and avoiding interaction with others. To me, at that point, it seemed extreme to pull my kid completely out of school, so we didn't do it right away. But I see now that it made sense. The situation was destroying his self-confidence. He was not doing well there.

Eliya: How do you explain Sammy's reaction to the change of structure in the kindergarten?

Alan: Sammy has a lot of anxiety issues which make him very sensitive to change. Any change can trigger anxiety in him. We became aware of Sammy's anxiety when he was two. He behaved in strange ways that we didn't understand. He would suddenly get really scared and wouldn't want to leave a place or wouldn't want to go somewhere. At that time we got very worried, because we didn't know what was causing this unusual behavior.

Sammy was reacting to the change in structure in the program which included a change of teachers. He just did not handle the changes very well. It was really unfortunate because he had been making good progress during the previous year.

Since we couldn't change the structure we thought the only option was to remove Sammy from the kindergarten.

Eliya: How did the kindergarten react to Sammy's behavior?

Alan: They wanted Sammy to have a psychiatric evaluation. They were always obsessed with these things. They thought maybe he was having a psychotic episode or something like that. We didn't want to do it because we didn't think that he really had anything wrong with him, but we agreed. Going to the psychiatrist turned out to be great.

Eliya: How so?

Alan: For a change the psychiatrist was a professional who listened to us. She wasn't the kind who was looking to label, as in "Oh, he's psychotic." We appreciated this psychiatrist's approach. We had experience with professionals who were just looking for proof of what they assumed was our son's problem. Once we were sent for a neuropsychological evaluation to test for autism. But we knew Sammy wasn't autistic. The psychologist said she couldn't conclude anything because Sammy was so distractible she couldn't run the tests that she needed. We paid almost $1,000 for that non-evaluation.

The psychiatrist that we were now seeing immediately understood the situation that we were in, and supported our decision to pull Sammy out of school. Her evaluation was very clear that there was no psychiatric issue and there didn't appear to be any communication issue. She recommended that Sammy be provided a "suitable framework to meet his particular educational needs." A "suitable framework" is a formal recommendation that directs the school system to find an educational program which is "suitable" to a child's particular needs.

Eliya: Until a "suitable framework" was found for Sammy what did you do with him at home?

Alan: We didn't do much with him. He watched a lot of TV. He was just home with us every day. When we "officially" took Sammy out of the kindergarten we were eligible for a private teacher to come to our house. At first I was very excited about it. It was three times a week for an hour and a half each time. But when the teacher finally showed up, I realized that the program was not set up to deal with kids like mine. It's set up to deal with situations where maybe a high school kid gets injured and can't go to school. The teacher who showed up was used to teaching much older kids and definitely not special ed.

But I said, "Okay, let's see what happens." But it was like a joke. You can't get a child into a learning mindset when he's at home. When he's home, he's home. He gets to run around and do whatever he wants. So it was very difficult for the teacher. It was a little funny to watch in the beginning. But you know, the teacher actually surprised me. He never learned how to get Sammy to sit down and seriously learn, but he managed to get some stuff done with him through playing and running around and things like that. But the whole experience didn't really work out.

Sammy was at home for four months straight. A really long time. The relief from the kindergarten was immediate: he stopped drooling and the anxiety disappeared.

At first we thought that all we needed was a solution to the problem of a six-year-old at home. But we realized that we were just babysitting a six-year-old who needed a learning program. He needed a structure which we didn't provide. It was not good for him and definitely not good for us. It was *extremely* difficult for us. Very stressful.

Eliya: What did you do when the home-school arrangement didn't work out?

Alan: We went looking for a school environment that we thought would fit Sammy. It wasn't until we got all the way up to the director of special education in the city that we were successful. She found a suitable framework for Sammy. How did we get all the way up to the director of special education in the city? I think the psychiatrist that we were seeing a couple of months before was instrumental in that happening.

The director arranged for us to see a whole bunch of special-education places, some of which we already knew were definitely out of the question. It turned out that the first place we went to visit was a program for kids where it's not clear what their issues are. They take children for a year during which they recommend what kind of program they think is suitable for them.

This school has tiny classes and one can wait a long time before a space opens up. But someone had just left the day before. My wife and I came in and we were saying, "This is the place for him! Why are we not here? Why didn't he go here this year?" And they took Sammy and it turned out to be great.

Eliya: Sammy made a change from being at home to a new school situation. How did he react to that change?

Alan: His time out of school was double the time of summer vacation. But he adapted quickly to being back in school. And he was so happy. He wasn't crying in the morning and he actually began to learn things. He started there this last March and now the year's almost over. But he has done so well that we feel as though he has had the whole year there.

Eliya: Given how well Sammy adjusted to the new setting, have you allowed yourself expectations for the transition to first grade?

Alan: Right now, in terms of expectations, I'm hoping that he will be mainstreamed. But right now I'm not too concerned about it. My wife also shares that feeling.

Look, some kids are just like this. We're lucky we're living in this time, because once upon a time, kids like this really struggled. It might be very difficult. It might take a long time, but I'm optimistic.

Eliya: How has all the focus on Sammy impacted on your relationship with your wife?

Alan: It probably did put a good amount of stress on our relationship, now that I look back, but I don't see that there were any negative consequences as a result of that.

I'm very relaxed and very laid-back. My wife tends to get worried very quickly. So somehow that worked. She was always the one who was concerned and wanted to consult with someone, and I was always the one saying, "Nah. Just leave it; it's nothing."

Eliya: How did your daughter react to her little brother?

Alan: OK. Emmy is three years older than Sammy so she grew up accepting how her brother behaved. When she was six Sammy entered the special education kindergarten. At that point she became aware of Sammy being different. So we began to explain to her certain things about him. But she continued to accept him.

Eliya: How does Emmy get along with her brother now?

Alan: They have a pretty good relationship. Emmy knows that Sammy has problems, that he's going to a special school, that he didn't talk for a long time. She actually talks about it very openly. Her teacher told me that in school Emmy talks openly about her brother.

Emmy has learned on her own to put up with a lot of Sammy's stuff. But now she's getting older and needs more time for herself, and for her friends. There is a certain friction between Emmy and Sammy because it's hard for Emmy to have friends over since a lot of times Sammy misbehaves in front of them.

Eliya: You have another son who is seven months old.

Alan: Yes. For many years, Sammy was the focus of our house. There's a reason for the six-year difference between the two boys. For us to manage having a baby before this would have been extremely difficult because Sammy was a handful. Also it would have been complicated for him if he had a younger brother or sister, say two years younger than him. At some point his baby brother would have been more advanced than he.

Eliya: Do you have any place inside of you that's just a little bit anxious as to whether your baby will also have a problem like his brother?

Alan: Yes, there's always that concern and there always was, all along. Even from before we knew that we were having another child. But we don't see it as a reason to not have children. What's the worst that's going to happen? You'll have another child that, even if they do have a similar issue, it's not terrible. I could imagine that for other people who have children with much more severe issues, it is a much more difficult question, but for me it's definitely not a big deal. I mean, look at Sammy now!

Eliya: What is it like with Sammy now?

Alan: In my eyes Sammy is doing great. Sammy's speech and communication skills have developed to the point that the psychiatrist has been able to converse with Sammy on several occasions. Sammy speaks and understands both English and Hebrew. We speak English at home so his English is better. He translates from English to Hebrew but often cannot find proper replacement words. At school he speaks and learns in Hebrew so he's improving there. There is still a delay in his speech development because he started talking so late, but he's improving.

He still has temper tantrums and is sometimes extremely disobedient. He knows how to push my buttons.

Eliya: What do you do when your buttons get pushed?

Alan: I have very tough skin. It takes a lot to tick me off. Overall, I can control Sammy, but that's not to say I won't ever get angry. Of course, I will.

Eliya: What have you done to keep things "normal" in your family?

Alan: A lot of acceptance. When it became clear to us that there was a problem and that it may take a very, very long time to resolve things for Sammy to get better, there was a good amount of acceptance of certain things that we couldn't change.

How were we able to accept it? In my mind, we didn't have a choice. Sammy is our child. So we do all we can do to provide for our children.

When we first started in the special-ed program, we spoke to someone who lives in the neighborhood who has a son with cerebral palsy and is in Sammy's school. She said it best: "Your job is to get your kid to do the best that he can. Even if it's not much, that's our job." My job is to give my children all the means and the best support to get them to be the best that they can be, whatever it takes.

Eliya: Did you ever wonder how come you are having this whole experience?

Alan: You mean like, "Why is this happening to me?" No. I'm not that kind of person. I don't like to even think about "why me?" I accept that it's me. For my wife also it's very much the same thing.

Eliya: What are the major challenges that you face now with Sammy?

Alan: Our son will be going into first grade. As far as expectations, I've learned not to have any, because it's unrealistic. We don't even have an exact name yet for his problem. I don't know if we're ever going to know what he has. Right now it's defined as "complex learning disabilities:" he doesn't learn things the way other kids do; he needs a different environment for learning, but he's absolutely able to learn. That's the label that the evaluation team gave him, and I accept that. That kind of label is okay with me because it doesn't mean anything. It's not like "dyspraxia," or whatever.

Eliya: What have you learned about yourself from being Sammy's father, Alan?

Alan: Rarely do I have time to sit back and think about it. A lot of times you just get caught up and all you have on your mind is what's going on right now, how to handle it, what's the right decision to make.

But thinking about it, I guess I learned that you can accept and you can cope and that you have the capabilities to deal with whatever challenges are presented to you. The way I understand it is that you don't really have a choice when you have a challenge like my son. You have to deal with it.

Eliya: What might fathers be able to learn from your experience raising Sammy?

Alan: What would I want people to learn from my experience? I think that acceptance is the most important thing. You really have to learn how to accept these things. There are some things you just won't be able to change. You have to do the best you can to get your child to be the best that he can be.

Eliya: No different than any other child.

Alan: Exactly. It may be a lot more difficult, but it's the same responsibility. You can't just dump it on the school: "You get my kid to wherever you can get him." There's a lot more involvement. A lot more.

Eliya: Thank you for being so open with me, Alan.

9
ZACK

Zack's only child was born with Down syndrome. For the first six months of her life Elana did not respond to either Zack or to his wife, Marcia. Professionals would not commit to what would explain Elana's lack of response. By closely observing his daughter and by doing extensive research, Zack diagnosed that Elana was PDD before the professionals did.

Eliya: As you were anticipating being the father to your first child, what were you looking forward to?

Zack: In the very early stage, I was thinking everything would be natural, and for lack of better words, we would have a, quote-unquote, "normal" child, a child without the extras that Elana now has. I never thought of having a special child when I imagined having children.

Eliya: Did you have dreams of having a boy or a girl?

Zack: I think I was hoping for a girl, because a boy would mean a circumcision, which would put me more upstage. With a girl you can sort of be in the background. I was definitely hoping for a fully healthy child.

Eliya: Did anything during the pregnancy suggest that Elana was not going to be a typical child?

Zack: During the pregnancy, she was remarkably quiet and moved very little.

In the fifth month, my wife went for a standard blood test, which indicated there was a small chance of abnormality. We said, "Okay, we'll take the chance."

At twenty-two weeks, the doctors wanted the very definitive amniocentesis test. But there's a risk to the fetus attached to the test so we didn't do it. Besides, whatever the outcome would be, we would still keep the baby. Both of us agreed no matter what, that would be our child.

The phenomenon of Down syndrome was not unfamiliar to us. The first child born to my wife's brother, some twenty-seven years ago, has Down syndrome. But because the child is so well integrated into their family, among all the siblings, we were not too apprehensive about the prospects of also having a child with Down syndrome.

Eliya: When there was the suggestion made that this child might not be a typical child, do you recall whether that altered anything for you in terms of your joy in looking forward to the birth?

Zack: Not at that time, because two different doctors indicated that the chances were very high that the child could be a normal child. One said there's only a one in six chance of an atypical birth, while the other doctor said there was a ninety percent chance of a normal child.

Eliya: How prepared were you for Elana's birth?

Zack: Elana was born prematurely, so the birth was actually very much unexpected. Just prior to the birth, Marcia was experiencing unfamiliar symptoms. We didn't know what was going on. My wife had called her sister to describe the symptoms and her sister said, "I think you better get to the hospital quickly."

We lived out on a farm at that time, and a local sheep farmer very kindly offered us a ride to the hospital. On the way to the hospital, he said, "Don't worry if anything happens. I've had tons of sheep give birth in this pick-up truck."

Labor was rapidly progressing, and everything went much, much quicker than we had been prepared for by our birthing coach. She had painted everything rosy, but it turned out to be all rush, rush, rush.

Eliya: What was your reaction when you were told at the birth that Elana may have Down syndrome?

Zack: I couldn't believe it, and I thought that they must be wrong. The baby was not immediately whisked away after the birth. She remained with her mother for about ten minutes, enough time for Marcia to connect with Elana. She immediately saw that Elana had Down syndrome. Marcia recognized it, particularly through the swollen bit around the eyes. Elana was then taken away for observation and tests. Marcia said to me that for her it was love at first sight. That settled it.

Eliya: When you saw that your wife immediately bonded with your daughter, then you were also settled?

Zack: Well, not entirely. I remember following the doctor at close range. When he took Elana, I wanted to be there with her, but I was not allowed into the room. I was struggling a bit with that. When he came out, he said it was definitely Down syndrome. I asked him, "How do you know?"

He said, "On at least fifty counts."

I said, "Okay, tell me." But I didn't want to accept it and was kind of fighting the facts. He told me a number of signs, which he showed me as well.

Eliya: How did you deal with this proof that your daughter had Down syndrome?

Zack: I just said, "Okay, what next? How do we take it from here?" I couldn't challenge it anymore. The doctor also told us that Elana was very yellow, and had to be under UV lights. That lasted for twelve very hard days.

Eliya: What made it so hard?

Zack: We were only allowed to be with our baby for the time it took to give her twenty-five milliliters of expressed breast milk. All the rest of the time she had to be under the UV lights. And even when we could hold her and give her the milk, it was difficult because she would hardly drink. It would take up to fifty minutes to finish that small amount.

Being in an incubator and under the lights all the time, our not being able to connect with her and having to leave her there alone every day, and spending the Sabbath in the hospital—this was a terrible way to start out with our new baby. Most difficult of all was not being able to connect with Elana. We got no direct response from her even when we held her. It took at least six months before there was any sign of eye contact or response to our touch.

Elana was also diagnosed with moderate to severe hearing loss. And she had a hole in her heart which would require a surgical procedure to close a heart valve. This may all have contributed to the fact that she was a very docile child, and we were not part of her world for a long time. That was certainly the toughest part.

Eliya: How did you cope with that?

Zack: It's hard to say. We lived one day at a time and prayed a lot.

Eliya: I know you received a lot of clinical information about your daughter, but did anyone ever say something encouraging to you?

Zack: The nurses in the room with the incubator and lights were quite encouraging. They wanted us to hold the child, help feed her, and talk to her.

In the first ten days, we had a lot of support from friends who were close to us, friends in our community, and friends from outside Jerusalem who called us up or came especially to visit with us. There was a young couple with one child who lived in the South, and they came with a lot of food and gave us encouragement in many ways. And they came again before Elana went home.

Now in retrospect, I see how tremendously important it is that people get support in the early stages. Once you have a foundation of emotional support, the pain doesn't knock you over. We could pick ourselves up with the blessings we received, and carry on.

We had gone through quite a bit, crying together, praying together, and receiving encouragement from people who have a living faith.

Eliya: How did you choose the name "Elana"?

Zack: I think the name Elana emerged through all that had gone on since the birth. Elana has the meaning of "light" and "mercy." We felt that G-d wanted us to see to it that our daughter would be a light, a blessing for everybody around her. That's one of our prayers that has been answered in a terrific way.

It took us ten days to find the name and in the very end we saw that it was all from Heaven. I don't think that my wife realized that her great-grandmother was Elana. We had talked it over with Marcia's mother, who gave us all the details of the family names, but we didn't have these family members in mind when we named our daughter.

Eliya: It sounds as if you traveled a great distance in just a very few days, from when you didn't want to accept that your daughter had Down syndrome to seeing her as a light for everyone around her.

Zack: That's right, and my wife probably came a much longer distance than I did. For me, it was still more head knowledge. For my wife, it was heart knowledge. She knew with the heart. For me, it was: "Okay, I'll go along with it."

Eliya: You say that you were relating to the situation primarily through "head knowledge." What was your "heart knowledge"?

Zack: During the first two years, I probably never shared my "heart knowledge" with my wife, because I felt it was not right to give her the pain of my pain.

My pain came from not knowing what I could expect from my child. Before the birth I had great hopes and aspirations for the child I would have, but now I didn't know what I had.

Remember, that for six solid months, Elana did not respond to our contact with her.

Eliya: How did you eventually find out "what you had"?

Zack: A unique clinic for children with Down syndrome at Hadassah Hospital at Har Hatzofim in Jerusalem was a great help for us. They gave us super medical help. We were living up in the Galilee and would travel to Jerusalem three times a year to see Dr. Taylor, the clinic's director. He related to Elana as though she was his own child.

As we received real information about Elana I began to feel relief from my pain of not knowing what to expect.

In the beginning stage Dr. Taylor gave us the encouragement that with additional time, Elana would respond more. At that point, we only knew she was Down syndrome; we did not know yet that her lack of response came from other challenges that our daughter had. When Elana was three and couldn't walk, Dr. Taylor said, "Not one of my patients has ever left the hospital not being able to walk. You have to be very patient." Elana started to walk on her fourth birthday. Thank G-d, today Elana can run, climb, swing, and walk up and down stairs.

We also went twice a year to the Feuerstein Institute, a renowned institute for children with delayed development, where Elana's speech and occupational development were evaluated. We always went back home encouraged by the evaluation and the tools they gave us to work with Elana.

Eliya: How did you try to make contact with your baby?

Zack: We held her, but we couldn't get any response from her. There was hardly any arm movement. Her eyes were never looking at us.

Eliya: How long was it before you could explain Elana's behavior?

Zack: When she was three years old, doctors confirmed a diagnosis of "mild PDD" [a label describing behavior on the autism spectrum]. It turned out Elana was not your typical child with Down syndrome.

Eliya: Were you surprised when the doctors confirmed a diagnosis of PDD?

Zack: No. By that time we had done quite a bit of research via the Internet. My wife came across a book called *Fine Motor Skills for Children with Down Syndrome*. This book was a very good yardstick to see where our Elana was holding compared to others her age. Our concern was raised when we noticed that even at the lowest level of developers, Elana did not make the mark in a number of areas.

That is when we really started to search the Internet with questions based on our own observations of Elana. I think we were both very much into it. We had collected questions about Elana over those three years and we searched for answers to all of them. At the end of our researching we said, "We're not medical people, but this is what we've come up with. Let's go now and ask the medical people questions."

Eliya: What happened when you began to ask questions?

Zack: In order to be accepted into the kindergarten in Jerusalem, Elana had to undergo a psychometric test. This test was going to be conclusive regarding Elana's mental state. I made a recording of the briefing we received after the test with the doctor who interpreted to us the test results. I had to press the doctor for her answer. I asked directly, "Listen, doctor, is Elana PDD?"

To this day, I still don't know why there was silence. But there was silence, and then a kind of under her breath "yes," as if she had said something so terrible and shocking that we would run away from it and leave Elana over there to be picked up by somebody else. I have no idea what that doctor was thinking.

When we finally received the doctor's diagnosis of PDD, I was very angry with the establishment and the medical world. I felt it should have been noticed much earlier. I still believe that there were plenty of indications that more was involved. Why didn't anybody say: "We think we're dealing with something more than just Down syndrome, and you better be prepared for it."

Eliya: How did having the PDD label change things for you?

Zack: Both of us were very relieved because we finally had answers to our questions, especially questions about Elana's lack of response.

Why is Elana holding this piece of string in her hand and dangling it all the time? Why is she doing this repetitive-motion thing? Why does she at times not want anyone to even come near her, as if we are invading her airspace? Why is she forever closing all the drawers and cupboards in the house? Why is she pushing the front door closed? Why doesn't Elana look at things—or at us for that matter? There was a whole list of things that we couldn't figure out.

Eliya: After that diagnosis, were you then able to start to work in a different way with Elana?

Zack: Yes, but not immediately. Maybe there had been something of our not wanting to acknowledge it, because when you acknowledge it, you have to deal with it. We had to get used to the new information, but eventually we came to accept this new reality. We began to understand that someone with PDD wants a small world and doesn't want to look at people. It's too scary.

Once I said, "Okay, she has PDD," then others came forth with, "Okay. Now, here's what we can do." That's how it was.

Eliya: Did you know how to go about getting the kind of support Elana needed?

Zack: Up North where we lived at the time we had a terrific social worker who really helped us get all our needs met with Elana. There was also a support group for the parents of Elana's kindergarten which my wife attended.

Eliya: How has it been for you watching Elana's growth and development?

Zack: Actually, if I sit down and chart a graph of my emotions since Elana's birth you would see that every period is unique. Every time Elana makes progress, my graph goes up. When she sinks a little bit, so do I. Then suddenly she peaks. Peak and sink, peak and sink. But it keeps climbing up, and every time there's a new victory.

She was unique at the very beginning because she hardly moved around. In the first year she began to move a little. She didn't roll, but she was on her back moving an arm or a leg. Slowly she could move a little bit more, and make sounds. In the beginning, we didn't hear any sounds—not even crying or laughing.

Eliya: With all the peaking and sinking, what has kept you going?

Zack: I think it was sheer faith and the belief that this child with all her challenges was who G-d wanted us to look after. It was not only for Elana, but it was for our benefit as well. It was that knowledge which kept us going when it could have been trampled and stamped upon because of what we saw happening with Elana.

Eliya: What have been the biggest challenges for you?

Zack: You have to work on trusting G-d. It's not as if somebody says something and at that moment when you hear it, you take it to heart and you run with it. Rather it's something like the *manna* [the spiritual food from Heaven that G-d gave the people in the desert], which you couldn't store up and it had to be replenished every day. You have to work on building faith.

But the progress is not a constant progress. It can peak and sink. Just like with Elana. There are those periods where you have to draw from a different source, rather than from what you see.

Eliya: Have you looked for external sources of support?

Zack: When we lived close to Kiryat Shemona, Marcia went to the Hebrew-speaking support group and found it helpful. Also, because Elana went to a special-needs kindergarten, we met parents of the children. I think Marcia got the most support from talking with them.

Eliya: Was there ever anything offered to you?

Zack: No, not that I needed it; I think Marcia needed it more. Her life is much more intertwined with Elana than mine. And I think that's because of the difference between male and female. A man just goes his way and he does his job, and whatever. For the mother, it's much more intense.

I had support in a different way. I would talk to people who were great in stature, who had a very firm understanding of our walk with G-d, and they shared the spiritual wealth they had. That was my support. I'm not such a great one in sharing emotional support; that's probably why I never look for a group.

Language was another factor. Marcia is better at speaking Hebrew than I am and that makes a difference.

Eliya: What's going on with Elana today?

Zack: Today Elana is a very responsive child. When we take her to her kindergarten or summer camp, everybody knows her; she's the star of the show. She's going to graduate this summer from kindergarten so she can go to first grade plus. They call it "plus" because it's special. That's what we say DS stands for, *Darn Special*.

Of course, now that we know her diagnosis of mild PDD, it helps us also to find the right place to go to. It isn't easy, because on a number of levels, she's behind. On other levels, she's much more advanced, so we've got a very mixed bunch.

Elana is in the school program at the Feuerstein Institute in Jerusalem. So far her being there is a great success.

The professionals at the Institute tell us that Elana has the ingredients within her to suddenly blossom and become a high-functioning child. It's hard for me to comprehend that. After all, it was just three years ago for the first time that she was able to sit at the table and do something for a few minutes at a time. Now she can sit and learn for longer periods of time. So I shouldn't limit myself.

Eliya: Do you work with her?

Zack: In a sense, yes. I play with her when I come home from work. Our play is often rough-and-tumble, and she loves that. But it's problematic, actually, because that is what she knows and likes to do with her friends, and she cannot communicate except by pulling somebody over.

Eliya: What is Elana's health like?

Zack: I think her energy levels are down when she is full of mucous, which up till now has been a good part of the year. There are a few spells when she is free of everything, and then she is a very bouncy child, who doesn't mind walking up the stairs and running down the street. But those periods are few, unfortunately, which means that Marcia has to lift her a lot, if she has the strength for it. At twenty-two kilos, Elana can be a strain on her parents. Otherwise, she just sits and eventually will drag herself up, but that could take a half-hour wait.

Eliya: Do you give Elana academic training?

Zack: We have tried to read with her, but without success. Since we have purchased an iPad we use this as a tool to get her familiar with counting, colors, and educational videos. At times we sit down in the evenings prior to going to bed to do things to stimulate her fine motor skills.

Eliya: What is it like with Elana out in public?

Zack: It is a big challenge because Elana does not like visiting new places or being in large crowds. She used to like coming to synagogue for the food and drink Sabbath morning after services, but not for the last twelve months.

People will say "Hello, Elana," but very often she does not acknowledge people who greet her. If she's sitting and holding something in her hand, we will first have to take it out of her hand, because that's the only way to break the spell of the PDD world and move her into the real world.

She can either get upset about that, or just simply not respond. Sometimes, she says, "Bye!" which means "Go away from me. Go out of my world. I don't want anybody around." She says "Bye-bye" when she goes to the doctor's office, a place where she doesn't want to be.

Eliya: Elana is your only child.

Zack: It is G-d's choice. We see this as G-d's way of saying, "Okay, it would have been nice for Elana if she had siblings, but I don't know how well her parents would have handled it."

Eliya: It sounds, Zack, as if you and your wife closely work together to raise Elana.

Zack: Yes. My relationship with Elana has helped build my relationship with my wife. Sometimes it looks as if we have nothing else to talk about. We had a situation where Marcia had to travel to Canada for nine days to visit an elderly relative who was dying.

I had to fend for Elana and myself here, and it went remarkably well. There were a whole lot of routine things that were always done by her mother, which were now done by her father, and Elana never complained. But she did show mild signs of her missing her mother.

Elana's delight was to see her mother again. When she saw her, Elana said the word "Mummy" for the first time. The word must have been taught to her in kindergarten during those nine days. That was the best present anyone could have given my wife.

Eliya: Tell me about Elana's progress to date.

Zack: Elana's vocabulary is ever increasing. We see that she very much understands English and Hebrew. She can now communicate in one word what she wants, for example, "water" if she wants to drink, "food" if she is hungry, "park" if she wants to go to the park, and "bed" if she is tired. Her ability to ask for a food item in a three-word sentence is definitely taking shape. She has her way of joining in with us saying the grace after meals. It is just wonderful. Elana also has the ability now to follow commands like "Put this in the trash." She will take the rubbish and put it in the bin. Or, "Pick up the plate you threw." She will get up and pick it up.

Elana has become more and more affectionate towards her parents, teachers, friends, and anyone she feels safe with. She greets you with a "hello" and acknowledges your "hello." She will say "bye-bye" at the right time when she wants to leave.

Elana's walking has now turned into running and she is now jumping on the trampoline, where she has developed a very good sense of stability. I made her a rope ladder, which she loves to climb onto. When it comes to swinging on the swing, she scares her mother back into the house so she won't have to watch Elana reaching "great heights."

Eliya: Do you think about Elana's future?

Zack: Yes, but I don't like to think about it. I see her future integrated with our future, and we have Elana as a job for the next however many years. We're not the youngest of parents, and thoughts of caring for Elana when we are older is not a nice prospect, to be honest, but we have to live with it.

When it comes nearer the time that we have to start making decisions, with G-d's help we'll make the decisions. But at the moment we enjoy the life we've got here now. Otherwise, you worry yourself sick, and that does not help anybody.

Eliya: Thank you so very much for this interview, Zack. You have been so open and articulate about your experiences.

Zack: It helped me, Eliya, to go back over old things. When you go back in memory, you can actually recall emotions like happiness, sadness, and everything.

Thank you.

Eliya: You're welcome, Zack.

10

GARY

After having two of their own children, Gary and his wife begin a foster care of a newborn with Down syndrome. They named him Noah. The foster care lasted eighteen years. In that time, two of Gary's natural children required special attention because of their severe acting-out behavior. Gary speaks frankly about the challenges to himself and his family of raising three children with disabilities.

Eliya: When did you decide to foster a child?

Gary: We had two kids at the time. The oldest was then about two and a half years old.

Eliya: What was your motivation for wanting to foster a child with disabilities?

Gary: I'd worked in an institution where I saw people who had very limited opportunities. It was something of a dream to be able to take someone out of that.

Eliya: Was it a dream that you and your wife shared?

Gary: To be honest, I think I pushed her into it. She agreed to go along with the trip, but it was my impetus.

Eliya: What choice did you have about what special need your foster child had?

Gary: We were referred to a social worker from the municipality. We asked, in general, what was involved and how it worked. This social worker was looking for a family to care for a child with Down syndrome and heart defects and all kinds of complications. She asked if we would be willing to take that child, but we backed off and said no.

Eliya: How did it come about that you later agreed to foster-care a child with Down syndrome after having first declined to do so?

Gary: About six months later, the social worker rang us again. We hadn't had any contact with her in all that time. She said, "I don't know what you're doing, but I've got this new baby." We were hesitant, but we went into it.

Eliya: Once again, what motivated you to want to raise a child like this? It's not a typical thing to do—and a big responsibility.

Gary: Well, it's not entirely a big responsibility, because you're fostering, you're not adopting. Fostering is a different ball game. If you don't want to do it anymore, you can say, "I'm sorry, I can't do this anymore." You also get money, not a great deal, but you get money to help you, so it's not going to cost you. And there's a system of social workers and administration behind you to help make it happen.

So it's not the same as adopting, where they say, "Congratulations, here's your baby and have a nice life." You get a lot more support and structure with fostering. Plus, you've always got a way out, which is very comforting.

Eliya: So you were ready now to take on the responsibility?

Gary: We said, "You know what? We don't know if we can really do this. Let's do a three-month trial." And the authorities said, "Great. Do a three-month trial."

After three months, we learned that Noah needed to have a heart operation. We said: "It's kind of not fair in this very messy, medically intensive period to pass him over to somebody else. So we'll keep going. We'll keep him for another three months until after the operation. Then we'll decide."

We took him through the open-heart surgery, four hospital admissions for different infections, lots of medically intensive stuff—like twelve doses of four different medicines every day—and constant medical supervision. Once we got that far, we found that my wife was pregnant with number three. By now, Noah was much more a part of the family. So we simply kept going.

Eliya: Let me just go back to my original question so you can elaborate. What was your personal motivation for fostering a disabilities child?

Gary: If I look back and I'm honest with myself, I see a lot of motivations. I think one of them was not entirely altruistic. People do all kinds of things to hear someone say, "Oh, wow, that's really impressive!" It makes you feel kind of special. *I'm doing something which most people don't do, and it's a big deal.*

I took Noah to the doctor for the first time, and the doctor shakes his head and says, "Wow! There are all kinds of good deeds, but what a good deed this is!" I kind of pat myself on the back, my chest puffs out, and I think, *Yeah, I really am doing something special.*

It's an opportunity to do something that makes a difference with your life, to significantly influence somebody else, and to be recognized for that.

Another motivation came from the fact that I'd worked in an institution where sixty people were living in one big building. I'd seen all these people who could have been functioning daily at a more independent level. There were lots of them who were capable of going to the kitchen, making themselves a sandwich, and taking care of themselves, but there was no open kitchen available because it was just too chaotic to run it like that.

I'd worked with all these sixty people for two years, feeling as though I was doing very little for them. I thought that if I could just take one of them and focus on him that would be more effective in changing lives.

Then there are more mundane reasons. We had space in our house. My wife wasn't working outside of the home, and the municipality gave money for doing foster care. They deliberately don't give you a lot of money, so that people won't want to do it *for* the money. But for us it was additional income.

If they hadn't given me the money, I don't think I would have taken in a foster child. I had to at least cover his expenses and have something left over.

Eliya: What was it like for you to bring another child into your home?

Gary: First of all, when we did it, we were quite naïve, and we thought, *We'll just do this thing for a trial period.* But then, to actually walk into a hospital on a Sunday morning with an empty baby basket, go into the nursery, look at the baby, and say, "Okay, we'll take him," and then go outside and get into a taxi and bring him home—all this happened without any pregnancy beforehand and without really knowing the child. We'd seen him only once, and we'd thought about it for a week or two, and it just sort of ended up happening. Then, all of a sudden he's there on your lap while you sit in the taxi, and then you're bringing him through the front door. That's really something that you don't forget.

Giving birth to a baby is disruptive on an emotional level, and to get a new baby instantly is even more so. I was more gung-ho and prepared for it, but my wife was much more hesitant. "Well, this is your idea," she said to me, "so you're going to be doing a lot more of the work with this one."

Eliya: How did your other two children react to having a baby suddenly brought into the house?

Gary: The other kids weren't old enough to really understand. For them it was, "Well, babies just come along, don't they? So, he's another one." They didn't quite get it.

Eliya: How did your wife feel about the addition of this child?

Gary: I think that in terms of our relationship, there were times when she felt that it was quite unfair. On top of caring for our two own children, the older being only two, she now had a child to care for who needed extra-special attention.

Eliya: How did you respond to your wife's feeling that it was unfair?

Gary: I took over the burden of care for Noah, much more than with the other children. There were four hospital admissions in the first six months of his life. Antibiotics, numerous doctors' visits for all kinds of checks, arranging all these medications, and coordinating all this medical stuff. I did it all.

Eliya: How prepared were you for your new baby's health issues?

Gary: We knew that our son had a hole in his heart. But before they could perform the operation, we had to get him healthy, get him fat, get him strong, and keep him alive, with this huge hole in the middle of his heart. We had to care for him as best we could for six months until he was ready for the operation. They couldn't do it earlier because he was too small.

On top of that, he had a lung infection, and then an eye infection, and then another lung infection, each one of which required that he be in hospital for a few days. That took a lot of doing, and it was always me in the hospital with him; which meant that my wife was home alone with the other two kids.

Eliya: Did you have any regrets about taking Noah into the home?

Gary: Not regrets like: "We can't do this anymore; this is really bad." But we did have thoughts like: "Maybe this wasn't such a good idea." When you're waking up in the middle of the night and the baby's screaming, there are plenty of moments when you think maybe this wasn't a good idea. But not regrets like: "I'm going to ring up tomorrow and tell the social worker we can't do this anymore." It didn't get that far.

Eliya: How did your parents and in-laws react to you having taken in a special child to raise?

Gary: When it came to my parents, I called my father and heard him writing down: "Okay, you're fostering a baby with Down syndrome. Okay, heart defect. Okay, he might very well die in the middle of all this. Okay..." So then he says to me, "Okay, well I'll tell all that to your mother, and you do your best." They were basically accepting and encouraging.

And then I rang up my in-laws to give the same news. While I had hoped it was going to be a conversation similar to what I had with my father, I got: "He's got WHAT?! And you have to do WHAT?! And he could WHAT?!" Complete rejection, and no response except for their belief that this was a very, very bad idea.

But eventually they also came around, as they have done with a lot of the other "bad ideas" that we have surprised them with during our married life.

Eliya: Now you had a new challenge: how to respond to the reactions of your family. How did you handle them?

Gary: I let them say their piece. I tried to listen respectfully. What was I going to do? As respectful and polite as I tried to be, I wasn't going to give up on the baby on the basis of their opinions. So we continued on.

Eliya: How did their attitude change?

Gary: They came here to visit, they saw Noah, and they had a better understanding of what we were doing and why. They asked what would happen with Noah in the long term when he's an adult, and I said that fostering could end when we choose. I explained that when he would be aged eighteen or nineteen, the plan was to find some sort of community residential arrangement.

I explained to my father-in-law that Noah was eligible for financial aid and various support services up to age twenty-one.

My in-laws heard that Noah wasn't going to be a financial burden, which was a big concern of theirs, and that fostering him was something that was important to us.

Eliya: You have thought it best for Noah to move out of your house at age eighteen or nineteen?

Gary: Yes, I do think that way. Away from home, you're out in the world on your own, working in sheltered workshops or wherever you work, doing the best you can. But, of course, it's never going to be as supportive as it is when you're in the school system and living at home. I've always thought that it would be good for a child to still have that system of support from the school when he makes the transition to community living. And I strongly believe that it's not good to make the two changes—moving out of home and moving out of school—at the same time. I think that's a very bad idea. I don't know which one has to come first, and I don't know how much space there should be in between, but I definitely wouldn't recommend finishing school and leaving home at the same time.

Eliya: How has it worked for Noah?

Gary: Thank G-d, things worked out really well. At age sixteen he began living in a shared, supported community apartment. He's still going to the same special-ed school, so he's well taken care of.

Noah comes home once a week, and he's very happy to tell us how bad it is at this apartment, that every night they tell him he has to go to sleep, and every morning they make him get up and take a shower, and all these terrible things! He likes to complain and he often says he wants to come back and live "at home." But the next week he'll tell us that he's happy in "his home."

It's good for him.

Eliya: You have two other sons who have presented you with challenges. At what point did the other boys demand extra attention from you?

Gary: The other boys grew up pretty typically, and then in their adolescence, their disabilities became more pronounced and difficult. Up until that point, they kind of managed to scrape through and stay in a regular religious grade school. I also took them with me to a program for fathers and sons to learn together.

Eliya: Prior to adolescence, did they show any signs that they might require special attention?

Gary: I regularly went to the parents' meetings at school and heard whatever reports there were. Maybe I got called into school a bit more often than other parents. Maybe there were more incidents of truancy, or not being up to par with academic performance, and issues like that.

Eliya: Starting at what age?

Gary: There was an incident in first grade with Jeremy, my firstborn. He once picked up a chair and held the four legs in the direction of another boy, who slipped or was pushed and somehow managed to cut his face on a leg of the chair. That was serious, and Jeremy had to change schools.

Eliya: How did you react to your son having to change schools in first grade because of his behavior?

Gary: Something like this makes you look at the kid differently. You look at the boy and you think, *Wait a minute, what's going on here, what's happening here, how normal is this?* All boys can get into a scuffle, have a fight, lose their temper, push and shove, and things can go wrong and become excessive.

But when a child lacks awareness of the seriousness of his behavior, or lacks remorse for doing things like that, that's way more scary. That makes you concerned that things aren't alright.

You see these little things. It creeps up on you.

You see a few drops of rain, and then you realize that it's really going to pour down. You realize you're going to get wet here.

It creeps up on you.

Eliya: Were you able to find some advice and help?

Gary: At the time, I think I was deliberately trying not to put a professional diagnosis on what I saw with Jeremy. I didn't want to say that he needs to be medicated, labeled, or diagnosed.

Eliya: What was your concern about doing so?

Gary: I think that's just part of who I was. Maybe I didn't see it or didn't want to believe it. Looking back now, I deliberately didn't want to do the labeling.

Eliya: What did you think about yourself and your effectiveness in raising a son who had acting-out problems in school?

Gary: There's always that kind of guilt with a biological child. It's different with our foster son. We had done this great thing and taken Noah in. There's no shock of diagnosis, and there's no guilt. You're a great guy, and you're doing this great thing, and you know exactly what you're getting.

When it comes to my other two boys with learning disabilities, they're mine. I'm asking: "Is that from my side of the family, or my wife's? How much of that is about me? How much is that because of something that I've done or not done?"

Eliya: How frequently do you have these thoughts?

Gary: I'm trying not to have them, but they come up. I'm a person who's generally more focused on the practical issues. I think more about: "Here's a problem and what are we going to do about it?" More than philosophizing about: "Where does it come from? How does that make me feel?"

Eliya: What were your challenges with the other two boys?

Gary: There was a real question about putting Jeremy into an official special-ed classroom. I saw it as a mechanism so he could stay at the same school and have the school receive more resources for him. I felt it could be a good thing for the school to have more hours and resources to give him, so I let him be officially called whatever they wanted to call him. I didn't think he would really be paying a high price for the school to put a label on him.

Eliya: How did things go from there?

Gary: Jeremy made very good progress. He turned out to be one of the golden boys of the school that he went to and received a full high school matriculation. Then he served in an elite unit in the army after doing very well in basic training.

Eliya: How did his learning disabilities get taken care of?

Gary: I think the disabilities were mild. Also, he was given a lot of self-confidence and opportunities to grow, just by being in the school, which was very, very supportive. Nothing medical was done, and there wasn't any great psychological intervention.

Home was part of this positive growth process in so far as we tried to be supportive and establish reasonable boundaries. However, I credit the school for his success much more than I do myself.

Eliya: What about your other son?

Gary: With Mike, I credit myself more and have gotten more involved with him in the last number of years. I thought medication would benefit him and I pushed it, even though my wife was against it. I believe it has been very beneficial. Also, I established boundaries for him while putting a lot of effort into maintaining a relationship. I have tried to keep communication open with Mike to help him understand where he is and why we are doing what we are doing.

If we don't keep him at home with these boundaries, he's going to be with the wrong people, smoking cigarettes or whatever else they do in the streets. He's going to be walking around in the middle of town, late at night. If we don't put effort into defining boundaries and building a relationship, he's going to get lost.

There's a much greater danger that things are going to get worse with a boy like that. If you're not significant in their life, then somebody else will be, and it will probably be one of their friends who's equally lost, who thinks that all the dumb things that they're doing are a good idea.

If you don't get involved, you're really living a very dangerous situation.

What we're talking about is more serious than just special ed or Down syndrome. With a boy with Down syndrome, if you don't get involved, maybe he turns into one of those people who has strange compulsive hand gestures or talks to himself in public. It's not going to be as bad as the life of a kid with learning disabilities who goes off the track and gets seriously messed up.

Eliya: So you consciously said to yourself, *I must be more involved with this boy.*

Gary: Yes, I had to be. There were more than four major incidents at school in less than six months. For example, in the study hall, Mike punched a boy in the chest and the boy collapsed because he couldn't breathe. In another incident, Mike got pushed onto another kid, then got up and started fighting with the other boy in a busy, crowded corridor.

Those are things that can happen in school every day. You can always get pushed and stumble and bump into people in a crowded boys' high school environment. But if you can't control yourself there, things are going to go downhill fast.

There were a lot more red lights and a lot more worry about not being involved enough when it came to Mike.

Eliya: You had three boys requiring special attention, followed by two daughters. What was it like during those early years?

Gary: It's not so simple to think back fifteen years ago and to remember how it was for me. For many years, though, it seemed stressful, overwhelming, and never-ending. There were quite a number of years when there were just a lot of little people in diapers, and meetings, and constantly a sense of never doing enough, never being enough, and never having enough time for it all. Plus, there was never having enough time for yourself after you've tried to do it all.

Eliya: How did you take care of yourself during all that time?

Gary: I don't know. In more recent years, I'm putting a stronger emphasis on taking care of myself and my mental health. I try to exercise, which I've learned is a big part of mental health. I take time for myself and put limits on what I'm going to do and not going to do for both my children and my wife.

I don't know how I got through it then.

Eliya: How did the girls react to their brothers? Were they supportive and caring, or was it a challenge to them also?

Gary: It's much harder to be the sisters of boys with learning disabilities than to be the sisters of typical boys. My girls were always saying to their brothers: "You've got your room and we've got our room, and keep away..."

The boys are going to be barging into your room, they're going to be telling you what to do, and they're going to be noisy and disruptive, much more than any normal boy. And as hard as it is for any girl to understand why boys are so annoying, it's even harder in this case. Especially for one of my sons it's been a major issue to find a way to maintain the peace with all the disruptive energy in the household. It's still a major issue today.

Eliya: What did you do about these difficult family interactions?

Gary: I don't remember specific techniques. I can't tell you about a book I read, a group I went to, an expert I consulted or a lecture that I heard, or an organization I was part of. I didn't follow any formal system. You try to divide and conquer and separate them.

Somehow I muddled through it.

Would it have been helpful to me to have advice from someone? It could have been if I was open to it. I don't know if I wanted people coming in and telling me how to do things according to other people's great ideas. I don't know how open I would have been to that. But having a place to ask questions and find support might have helped.

Eliya: Did you ever find such a place?

Gary: We did get some relief from a project where university students come and they take your kid with disabilities out for one afternoon a week. In return, they get a reduction in their student fees. We had that for our Noah. Things like that were very helpful.

A preschool in the neighborhood integrates typical and disabled children with disabilities. They had a sibling support group. Any activity that takes the kids out and takes the pressure off for a few hours is always very welcome. It doesn't matter which kid it is, because even if one kid out of five, six, seven, or eight kids is kept busy that's very significant.

It was helpful when we went to the annual conference of a local organization which advocates for Down syndrome. Plus, I have a professional background and could talk to people at work about special education and its unique problems. As a father, what I didn't have was a specific support group with a shoulder to cry on.

Eliya: How might a support group have helped you?

Gary: Actually, I don't know if I would have wanted to hear anybody else's great ideas. I like to have my own great ideas, like my idea of making sure the child doesn't transition from school and home at the same time. I understand the issues that apply to my Down syndrome child, but I'm a bit more in the dark when it comes to my other boys because I have less professional background concerning their learning disabilities.

Maybe that's part of what pushed me to keep them in the normal school system and keep pretending that they're pretty much all right. That became harder to do as they fell more and more behind academically.

Eliya: How did you and your wife work out the division of responsibility for caring for your children?

Gary: We developed an effective system of dividing things up. We determined that I was going to do this and she was going to do that, which is a lower form of teamwork, but we both knew pretty much what each of us was capable of doing. For Noah I had the professional background to get into the medical issues and the educational issues. It was pretty much for me to decide which kindergarten, which school, which communication system, which types of interventions, and which sort of plan for the future. That helped in terms of expectations, in terms of keeping the peace, and that helped in terms of the overall plan. As we went through all of these challenges there developed a greater sense of shared experience. These experiences worked to strengthen our relationship.

Eliya: What were some of the experiences which strengthened your relationship with your wife?

Gary: One was the four major hospitalizations of baby Noah in less than seven months, including open-heart surgery. And that all happened when my wife was pregnant. Later on, when Noah needed extensive dental treatment, fillings and whatever, a general anesthetic had to be administered. Given his heart surgery, he was required to have a cardiac specialist check him before any dental work was done. So the whole thing becomes much more involved than simply going to the dentist.

Going through all that together does tend to strengthen a relationship. There's this shared sense of journey, accomplishment, and pride that we were able to keep the ship afloat somehow, no matter how much on a day-to-day basis we felt that the ship was pretty leaky.

Eliya: As your sons developed, how did your relationship with your wife change?

Gary: In the last few years there have been a lot of changes, with a lot of weight being taken off. Jeremy is married. Mike is now in the army; he comes home once every few weeks and so he has one foot out the door. Noah is now living in an apartment in a supervised environment. So in the space of two years, three out of the eight children have left.

Next year, Number Five is going to live in a dormitory at school, which will be a big change; he's also a heavy-maintenance customer. That should be, with G-d's help, a major step in finding a happy ending for him, or rather a happy beginning.

Our youngest child is now five, so there are no more diapers and no more nursing. He goes off to kindergarten each morning. There is nobody at home for half the day, so there's this significant freeing up of my wife's life, and our life together. That fits with the pattern I've heard about—that the first twenty years of marriage are usually the hardest. Once you get past those years, things can ease up quite a lot.

I can't say I've got a model relationship and ideal marriage, by any means. There are a lot of other issues besides the disabilities of those three boys. The reason why I can sit and talk to you now and I can even address these issues is because the hardest part is over. That's really the feeling. There are still plenty of days when you feel like, "*Oh my*, this is still very hard." But even on a hard day now, you're at a higher place. You're higher up on the curve, so you never feel like it's as hard as it was.

Eliya: How would you describe how raising these challenging children has changed you?

Gary: Everybody gets older and more mature. Everybody gets a little more understanding of themselves with time. How I've changed? I don't know how much of the change I can attribute to them or to my growing into the role of being a father.

Eliya: Do you feel you've achieved the goal you had in bringing a foster child into your home?

Gary: No, no, no. I started out with this great idea that I was going to take this boy and mainstream him. I was going to put him through the regular school system with whatever support he needed, and he was going to reach such a wonderful, incredible level, that he was going to get a real job in a real environment. That didn't happen.

Instead of being mainstreamed, he went through special education, and he doesn't look like he's going to get a real job in a real environment. He'll be working in some sort of sheltered workshop or other supportive situation.

I had this whole great idealistic plan which wasn't entirely based on who he was, but on what I thought he should be or could be. Maybe I was not realistic.

I went to lots of meetings of a local organization which advocates for children with Down syndrome and their parents. I always saw a correlation between the parents who push harder—who really work to make it happen for their child—and the kids who get there and become more independent. If not fully independent, then at least whatever level the child is, the child gets pushed up a notch. That was very clear to me.

Parents who push and know how to make it happen get a return on their investment. The more you invest, the more you get back. With these kids with disabilities, it's not always about what their level is, since very often they don't have a strictly fixed level of disability. However, sometimes there *is* a fixed level of disability and these kids will never learn to read, no matter how hard you try.

Eliya: How have you reacted to not being able to realize your high ideals?

Gary: You feel different disappointments at different times, and you deal with them one by one. First we were disappointed when Noah finished special-education kindergarten, and he wasn't going to go into a regular first-grade class. That was a bit of a blow. Slowly, slowly you destroy your ideals, and you build with the pieces that are in front of you.

Eliya: While your boys were demanding so much of your attention, how were you being a father to the girls?

Gary: The girls are perfect. You have little incidents, but you never have to worry. One went off to a boarding school. She had her mixed-up teenage years and built herself pretty much independently. I come from a family where the parents are pretty much hands-off in terms of who you want to become and how you want to run your life. We're not into micro-management, and the girls decided on their own path.

Eliya: Are you saying that you never had to do too much with them?

Gary: We were involved but we weren't directive. And when we did offer advice, we were supportive. My oldest daughter, Naomi, opted not to do National Service. I thought, *You know what? Okay.* Now the second daughter is telling me that she's thinking of going into the army. I think it's a bad idea, but am I going to scream and shout and try to stop it? Could I stop her from doing it? Probably not, and by resisting her, I'd probably make it even worse.

Naomi wanted to get professionally certified instead of doing National Service, and then she wanted to get married. I sort of put on the brakes on her getting married at that point. I said, "We can't help you very much financially. I think it's important to get a driver's license. As for a profession, you probably want to finish your course and get certified in something where you can work. Because if you're not certified in something these days, what are you going to do? Work in a supermarket?"

We're very limited in what we can do for her since we've got all these other young kids at home. We haven't got a car and don't have the financial means like some other parents. Naomi is married and we're very happy with the way things have turned out for her.

I don't know if it's typical that people worry about the boys more than the girls. Or maybe it's just something in my family that the boys have more issues than the girls. Both my wife and I tend to let things slide when it comes to the girls. For example, if Naomi doesn't want to do National Service, that's not so bad. But if Jeremy had said he doesn't want to be doing the army, I'd be thinking, *Wow! That's not going to be so good. What are you going to do if you're not going to go into the army? What is that going to mean for you in the future, and how's that going to affect your life?* We do worry more about the boys than we do the girls.

Eliya: Coming back to Noah, what has sixteen years of fostering a child with disabilities added to your family?

Gary: In engineering, there's a principle that to strengthen an arch of stones you add more weight to the top. That pushes the stones together and makes it a stronger structure.

So we added more weight and I'd like to think that it strengthened the structure. I can't say where we'd be if we had chosen the other path.

I see my children as being more sensitive to disabilities. My oldest daughter is now a medical technician. She went into a health field where she is giving to others. Another daughter is now doing National Service with old people. I think Jeremy wanted to join an elite unit in the army in part because it's all about self-sacrifice and giving and fulfilling, which he learned a lot about growing up in our family.

I think "giving" is a common thread throughout the family. We can't say specifically if it came from the fostering or not, but I think that is part of it.

Whether adding that weight to the arch also makes cracks in the building, it probably does. You lose out on certain things. But overall my family has been strengthened by having a foster care in our home.

Eliya: What has been the impact on you of fostering a boy with Down syndrome?

Gary: What did sixteen years of fostering a child with disabilities add to me? I believe that I've done something to be proud of. It's something that was good for me and good for the family. Fostering was something we were able to do and we did it.

Once you've taken a child through open-heart surgery and many different medical and behavior problems, you are able to assess a situation and say: "This is not a problem. It's a challenge and. we'll get through it." Things that used to freak me out don't freak me out anymore.

When my youngest son gets on his little beeper car and goes down the ramp in front of the building and smashes his tongue right before the Sabbath candle-lighting and I've got to put him in a taxi and take him to the hospital, or one of the kids tipping over cupboards and smashing things at school—it's just the next crisis to be dealt with and not something to really freak out about.

Problems are problems and they have to be dealt with, but nothing seems like the end of the world any more. You get vaccinated against those sorts of things. That comes with all parenting, but maybe more so with the big problems that come with a kid who has disabilities.

Eliya: Now that Noah lives out of the house, what kind of relationship do you have with him?

Gary: Noah lives in an apartment with other boys with disabilities in a different neighborhood. We call him quite often. It's a regular, fixed thing that he comes once a week and for whatever special occasions there might be. Even though now we're no longer his foster family, I am still "Abba" and my wife is still "Ima" and the family is the family, just like we have always been. He still is, and always will be, part of the family. His identity is part of our family's identity. That's always going to be there, and we encourage that and that's important for all of us. Even though that identity is not in any way legally recognized.

Eliya: Anything else you want to add?

Gary: If you're thinking about fostering, do it. You might think that you've got a busy life. I had two jobs and sometimes even three jobs at one time and I was still doing it. Or you've got too many kids, but we had seven other kids and we did it. Maybe you think that you don't have a background to be able to foster, but we didn't and we managed.

So you really can do it. And from what I felt in the very beginning and all the way through is a lot of Divine assistance. Your kids come to you—each soul comes from Heaven and those are your kids given to you with their own pluses and minuses and problems and talents, and that's obviously meant for you to deal with.

But even when it's fostering, I still felt that it was from Heaven, that it wasn't accidental that he ended up with our family. And when I looked at other kids in foster families, there's no way I could ever have imagined being a foster parent to them. It was only our son who came to us that ever really felt right, from the very beginning. I really believe that.

Eliya: Thank you, Gary.

11

JUL

Following a seemingly typical childhood illness, nine-month-old Avi had a seizure. A brain scan revealed that his optical nerve had atrophied, leaving him blind in one eye and severely impaired in the other. Thus started a dramatic change in the lives of his parents, Jul and Elaine Kornbluth. When they could not arrange an appropriate program for Avi in any of the local established schools they started a school that would. The school soon became the model in England for mainstreaming children with disabilities. For their contribution to Jewish education, Jul and Elaine were awarded the Israel Prize, the State of Israel's highest honor.

Eliya: Please tell me about your son.

Jul: Avi is a great guy. He is now thirty-eight years old and the father of six children; the oldest one is eleven, the youngest one is sixteen months. He has a gorgeous family. He works as a real estate manager and has also earned wide-ranging Orthodox Jewish rabbinic ordination. He lives around the corner, three minutes away. After finishing school in London Avi came to Israel to learn in yeshiva. He married a local girl. He loves it here and he has worked very hard to achieve what he has. He received his ordination in all areas except those that require sight.

Eliya: Why is his ordination limited?

Jul: Because Avi's vision is so seriously impaired that he has a 15-magnification set of glasses for one eye and the other eye has no vision at all. And he has to read things literally right up against his nose. But he was blessed with a tremendous memory, and he has a very good sense of hearing, which I suspect he has developed as compensation for the sight loss. He can recognize my voice across a crowded room. He will know I'm there because he's heard me say just one word aloud. And he will recognize anybody else's voice also.

He's mad into cars, although he's never driven a car on the street in his life. And he can recognize the make of a car by its sound.

Eliya: How did Avi lose his sight?

Jul: Avi's birth was normal and for the first nine months everything was fine. At about nine or ten months he became ill. It appeared that he was crying from pain in his ears. The doctor said he had an ear infection and prescribed antibiotics. After three courses of antibiotics Avi wasn't getting better at all. And we began to worry about him. We went out one Sabbath for a meal to my in-laws, and we left Avi with the babysitter. When we came back she said, "Oh, there was something wrong. He wasn't well and he had a seizure." We first thought that she had dropped him, but it turned out he really did have a seizure.

Following the seizure he suddenly lost all ability to move, all sight, all hearing, everything. He was completely lifeless. And we were very, very frightened. We took Avi back to the doctor, who said: "Don't worry about it; just give him some more antibiotics." But we lost confidence in this doctor because his prescriptions for antibiotics were not helping.

Over a period of about six weeks, Avi's functions came back one by one. Suddenly he started moving again, and to cry, and then to sit up. We weren't sure about his hearing, so we took him to specialists at the Great Ormond Street Hospital. They immediately suspected a genetic problem because my wife and I are third cousins. We knew that it wasn't a genetic problem. We actually had to prove with photographs and a short film that Avi was one hundred percent fine and normal from birth until the illness at nine months. We were becoming increasingly worried whether our son would ever get the right treatment.

The results of their investigation came back after several weeks. While we did not get a clear diagnosis, it seems that Avi had suffered encephalitis.

Following Great Ormond's conclusion of encephalitis, they sent us to Moorfields Eye Hospital for a brain scan. The scan revealed that Avi's optical nerve had atrophied, resulting in no vision at all in one eye and very little vision in the other.

Eliya: Can you recall how you reacted to hearing that your son had suffered such severe loss?

Jul: Well, we knew that he had suffered loss. By the time of the scan he was already a year old. For nearly three months we watched our baby develop. It was clear to us that he could hear, he could make noises, he could sit up, he was crawling around, just like any one-year-old could do, but he just couldn't see. We knew that, but we were hoping that just as his other abilities had returned to normal his sight would come back as well. But for about a year following the scan we were also living with the reports from the investigations at Great Ormond Street and Moorfields Eye Hospital, which reported that Avi's situation looked pretty bad.

Eliya: How did you maintain yourself in that year following the scan?

Jul: I think we were quite challenged by what we had to do. At that stage it was almost impossible to sit back and worry. And maybe the severity didn't even sink in, the long-term effect of what was going to be, which came later. We also had another child a year later, and that took up time. By the time Avi fell ill, my wife was already pregnant. We had to get things done. We had, luckily, a relative in the United States, a doctor, who shipped us information and books not easily available in England. It was before the days of the Internet.

Eliya: Did you have encouragement or support from other people?

Jul: Not really. We were on our own. I'm reluctant to say it, but both sides (who are now no longer with us), I think the grandparents to some extent, shied away from it. They didn't really want to know about it. I'm not sure whether they didn't know how to cope with it, or what to do about it, but we were left to our own devices. My mother didn't live in the same country as us. Elaine's parents lived around the corner, but they just didn't get involved, so we were very much on our own.

Eliya: Friends?

Jul: It didn't really come into that, to a very large extent. We didn't have that many friends then. It's only when you start getting kids into school that you suddenly start creating new groups of friends. At that stage, our oldest was three, just starting nursery school. We were a bit isolated. We weren't ready to share our problem with friends. I know it sounds crazy but we carried on to the outside world as if everything was fine. Maybe also because our own parents found it so difficult to accept, so we were concerned how others would react. But I, for one, didn't worry so much about the future. I didn't quite understand the significance of the diagnosis. I was hoping that he would recover fully, like he had recovered his hearing and his motor abilities. He had good dexterity, so I was hoping it would sort itself out.

Eliya: What professional advice were you following?

Jul: When Avi was two, we were lucky enough to meet another ophthalmologist at Moorfields Eye Hospital. She was a very aggressive woman, who said, "I will give him very powerful glasses, but you will have to work with him." My wife, based on the books sent by the relative in the US, learned that in the first three years after a trauma like Avi's, if you really work hard, you can actually regenerate a little, and possibly even a lot, of vision. In the book the doctor stated directly: "Do not accept the standard advice of the doctors, which says, don't strain his eye, rest his eye, don't put pressure on him; rather, do just the opposite: work his eye hard day and night and keep working on it."

Eliya: Yet the local doctors had given you a discouraging prognosis?

Jul: Yes, but the advice we got from this doctor in America was that we had a three-year window of opportunity to change things. And so that's what we were working hard at. My wife was working with Avi all the time. We had a lot of information from this eye specialist in America, the author of the book, on what to do and how to do it. The local eye specialist we saw said, "No, don't strain him, don't pressure him," but we had read that a nerve can be helped by stimulation, by getting it to work, so we just kept going.

The ophthalmologists in Moorfields were at first dubious, but eventually they said, "You know what? This doctor may be right. Persevere with it." And that's what we did.

Eliya: What kind of education did you arrange for Avi?

Jul: I think we sort of bumbled along and did as best as we could on our own until Avi was old enough for kindergarten. But instead of going to the Jewish kindergarten that our oldest son, David, had attended, Avi went to a small playgroup. He did well there.

A year ahead of when Avi was scheduled to enter primary school we began the application process. We started even earlier than usual because we knew we had to get the cooperation of the primary school to provide for Avi's needs. So we put our application in and began the discussions. And then the sky fell in.

The primary school, the only Jewish school in Golders Green, which was where Avi's older brother was, told us, "We're not taking him. We are over-subscribed, we are under pressure. We've got forty places and sixty applicants. How can we take on a problem child? He's going to be too difficult for us. Why should we take on a burden like that?"

And we said, "Well, there is no other Jewish school in the neighborhood. His older brother is in the school two classes above. And we will continue to provide an aide to sit with him. Why would you not take him?"

And they said, "No, we're just not interested in having any of that. What we recommend is that you contact the authorities, the education department, who will refer you to a school for the blind."

Schools for the blind in England are residential, non-Jewish, and tend to be out in the countryside, not in London. It would have meant placing Avi in a residential, non-Jewish, non-kosher place in Birmingham, a hundred miles from London. Just the thought of it was horrific.

Eliya: What was your reaction to hearing this from the school?

Jul: We were shocked that the Jewish school wanted nothing to do with our son.

And for a period of months, we were terrified of what would be.

We didn't feel that it would be right for Avi to be home-schooled, because he was doing so well in the playgroup. He was such a social animal, so well integrated with the other children. He used to go to their houses to play, they used to come to ours to play. Why should he be home-schooled? There was no question for us that a school setting was the only acceptable solution. And then my wife spotted immediately that there was a need to be filled.

She said, "Hold on a minute. There are sixty children fighting for forty places. Where will the other children go and what will happen to them?"

At that time, because the only Jewish primary school could not accommodate all its applicants, some religious Jewish children in Golders Green had to go to non-Jewish schools. So my wife started working with other people to find a solution to Avi's need and the larger need of the community.

Eliya: What happened next?

Jul: Elaine went to work. She organized a meeting with ten other parents who also couldn't get into the primary school. She arranged with them to go to the primary school and say, "We have other people besides ourselves. Will you start a second stream for us?" So my wife and the group met with the officials of the primary school and they said, "Yes, if you find for us all the money, but it will still be under our own auspices, which means we will still turn down your child and we will still give priority to the children in our local synagogue." They agreed to our funding a second stream, but many children living in other neighborhoods would still not be admitted, nor would Avi.

When my wife came back from the meeting she said to me, "This is just not going to work. They still won't take Avi. And he is not going to a residential school in Birmingham. I think we have to work hard and start our own school, independent of this one. There's no other solution."

You have to understand the English school system. You can start a private religious school program without anyone knowing about it, and be completely illegal, and hope to get away with it, and there *are* places like that.

But if you want to start a proper school in England, we have a system whereby, if you reach certain standards for the facilities, in the curriculum, and in the qualifications of the teachers, a religious school can apply to the government for funding the secular part of the program. This arrangement started in 1944 when the state nationalized all the church schools and created a partnership between the church and the state. In doing so they had to open the system for Jews as well, and our local primary school became what was at the time the only Jewish "Voluntarily Aided State School" in the country. My wife's idea of starting an independent Jewish school would mean establishing another formal partnership with the state.

Eliya: That sounds like a major undertaking.

Jul: It really was a major undertaking. We went to the government people and they laughed at us. They said, "We haven't given permission for another Jewish school in over twenty years. Why would we give one now? We have empty places in every single one of our state schools. You can't prove a need for another religious school."

And we went from authority to department to consultant, to everybody we could, and they all said it can't be done.

The director of education at the local authority in London proudly said to me, "We have not given permission to a new Jewish school in twenty-two years. We had to agree to an additional high school class, because we were taken to the European court, since there were three classes for boys and only two classes for girls, and because of the sex discrimination legislation, we had to concede a third class for the girls. But we did it only because they took us to the European court. We are not going to give you permission for a new school."

My wife worked day and night. I worked half-day and half-night. I had a feather-processing quilt factory and business which I had to maintain. Because in England women were not given the same respect as men, I became the trustee, even though my wife should have been since she was leading this effort, working at it literally full time. It certainly would not have happened without her efforts.

What followed next was a sequence of events which can only be described as Divine Providence. We met with the Chief Rabbi of England, Lord Jakobovits. He said, "The most important endeavor is Jewish education, and it's a great shame that there have been no new Jewish schools in twenty-two years. It's an embarrassment for the Jewish community." He gave us a blessing, and a lot of encouragement, and within two weeks the director of his office put us in touch with a gentleman who had access to substantial funds. The donor said to us: "Do it and I will do everything in my power to help you. I give you my blessing that it will succeed." Meeting this gentleman was a very big blessing, because we knew we wouldn't be able to pay for starting the school by ourselves.

We were then introduced to a fantastic lady who would become our first headmistress. We found a location for the school when my future sister-in-law was a young bride looking for a house. My wife asked if she could borrow the real estate agent's list. My wife instantly recognized a building where she had played as a little girl. It was a massive building sitting on one acre in the middle of the London suburb of Hendon. The site was an old-age home, and it was for sale.

So we went there, and we were nervous about saying we wanted it for a school, because we were sure that the seller would put the price up immediately. So we negotiated for it in the name of the bride and groom and bought it. So we had a head teacher, a third of our funding, and the premises all within two weeks of making the decision to start a school. That is truly help from Heaven.

This all happened in May. We had planned to start the school one year from the upcoming September, which would have been when Avi was of age to begin. We gave ourselves that much time to begin because the head teacher said, "Look, it's going to take time to recruit teachers, design the curriculum, do renovations to the building, and recruit a committee to look after things."

A month later, in June, there was a knock on the door and a lady stood there whom we had never met before, and she said, "I understand you're starting a school next September. Well, I have a child who hasn't got a place in a Jewish school *this* September. What are you going to do about it?"

And we said, "You can't start a school in three months. This is an old-age home at the moment. We've only just exchanged contracts; we haven't actually completed the purchase. And you can't start a school with only one child."

So she said, "Well, how many children do you need?"

My wife said to her, "Well, I'm hoping to restrict the class size to twenty-six. We need at least half a class."

So she said, "If I come back with thirteen children, will you start the school this September?"

Without knowing what we were letting ourselves in for, we said yes. And two weeks later the lady turned up with thirteen parents who said, "We don't have a school for our children." We met with all these parents one night in our living room at what must have been the noisiest gathering in London. Everyone insisted that we start in September. And we did.

We worked at it very hard. We recruited a team to be governors on the school board. One governor in particular was very good. He was a very nice electrician who was an appointed official on the local government town planning committee. We met him at a social setting and when he got really solidly drunk, he said, "You know, you chaps are really good, and nice people, and you really deserve this school. I'm going to get you your planning permission." He knew how to talk to the other local councilors, which he did by taking them out for drinks.

Unfortunately there was a very sophisticated lawyer on the planning commission who was not sympathetic to our cause. But luckily for us, Mr. Dipple, the electrician who was chair of the planning committee, finally said, "Well, it's going to be my decision whether you like it or not, councilor, so I'm going to grant the planning permission to this school." And that's what happened. We started with thirteen children.

We got temporary planning permission from the council to renovate the old-age home. They said to us, "Well, we don't want this school here, but we'll give you permission on a temporary basis for two years until you find something more appropriate."

Eliya: How did you start to build your school?

Jul: The director-general in the office of the Chief Rabbi of England said to us that all institutions in England work with a committee. You can't just be individuals. You have to have a committee. So we created a committee. We recruited friends whom we thought could help us. One chap knew about building construction, Mr. Dipple knew about lawyers, another chap knew about education. We had two or three people who would help us fundraise. So we recruited a team.

My wife said to me, "We're starting a new school. We've actually got before us a clean piece of paper. Let's think what we actually want here. It doesn't have to be a copy of the other school, plus Avi." That discussion started with me and my wife.

My wife and I established three founding principles, which we decided the trustees and anybody coming on board had to sign up on. Number one was that we would integrate children with disabilities into the school, as a matter of policy. Number two: we would teach the religious studies in Hebrew. Number three: the school would reflect a Zionistic orientation.

Interestingly for us, four years after we started, there was a professor of education in England, Mary Warnock, who published a book saying that every child is special, and called for integrating children with disabilities. The following year it became the law of England that all state schools, including Voluntarily Aided Religious State schools, have to integrate children with disabilities. The law had funding provisions and a process for implementation of the law.

Eliya: The concept of integrating, of mainstreaming, didn't exist before you started your school?

Jul: No. That's why the other primary school was able to turn us down and could say, "We don't want your child." It became law in 1984. And even after it became law—we specialized in it. We had children with Down syndrome, with sight problems, with hearing problems. Eventually, when integrating became law, other Jewish schools further out of London came to us and said, "Well, rather than duplicating services, let one school put in a hearing loop, let the other school do this, let the other do that..."

The established Jewish schools in London chose to send their children with disabilities to us. As the chair of governors of one very religious school, who himself had a child with disabilities, said to us: "You're good at it and we're just not going to do it." Sometimes parents would automatically put us as their school of choice, even if they weren't religious and weren't interested in the Jewish content of our program, because we were seen as the school for disabilities.

But whereas the school worked beautifully with regards to integration, we didn't want to become, by default, a special school. (It means a school only catering to disabilities rather than integrating special and typical children.)

Eliya: How you started the school and all the accomplishments the school has achieved is worthy of a lengthy interview on its own. The many honors you and your wife and the school have received speak to what you accomplished. Let's go back to Avi. Tell me about the program that you designed for him.

Jul: When Avi started in the preschool my wife said to the school's director, "Avi needs a helper. He's not going to be able to cope with the preschool by himself. " Eventually my wife found a helper after advertising the post. She was like an angel from heaven. She spent all day, every day, at Avi's side, helping him. They would do the work and learn letters, like all the children in the class. In England, we tend to start the schooling process when children are quite young. So at age three, children are already confronted with letters, and certainly at age four, they're into it. I think Avi had a happy time. He made friends, he was very popular. And he did well in the program.

I think that the main teacher in the preschool, a very lovely lady, quite liked Avi and quite liked the presence of his helper, who would also assist her with other things around the classroom. And we felt somewhat relieved that maybe this was the way forward. We felt that with the systems and the people in place to help, Avi would be able to cope with his limitations. We had to pay a lot of money for this woman, but it was worth it.

Luckily, this lovely lady stayed with Avi right through primary school. The big difference in the primary school was that the first few years our school didn't have Voluntary-Aided status; this was a separate fight to be eligible for state funding. We had to build a new building, we had to meet certain requirements, and we had to go to public consultations. I think it took us approximately three or four years until we got the Voluntary-Aided status, at which time the government started paying for the secular program. And they also paid for eighty-five percent of capital costs.

The way it works in England is that each child with disabilities gets what's known as a Statement of Special Educational Needs. In that statement are detailed provisions—for example, this child needs two hours a day help with motor systems; this child needs two hours a week of speech therapy—and the detailed provisions get funded by the government.

It was a lot of work to meet Avi's particular needs. Besides work at school we were doing work at home with him. Since I was working quite hard at that stage in my business, unfortunately I didn't do as much as I should have done with Avi. My wife was working very hard with him. The school installed a large-scale photocopier, A3 size. And so all his school work was photocopied by this lovely lady. Avi used to come home with these enormous workbooks; all his school and homework was done on A3.

We were making regular visits to Moorfields Eye Hospital, and they suggested we get Avi a closed-circuit TV so that he could actually read a book with the text enlarged on screen.

We worked very hard to get him all the equipment that was designed for his needs. He became a bit of a gadget freak. He loved anything like that. If there was a new binocular (optical device for increasing the field of depth) out, he had to have it. If there was a new closed-circuit TV out, he had to have it. And we did as much as we could to give it to him.

Eliya: Given the limitation of his sight, how did Avi develop socially?

Jul: Pretty good. He has fantastic hearing. So much so that for many years he was one of the top ping-pong players in his class, just on sound. Uncanny. But he could only play if there was one table.

He was a ferocious soccer player in school. He probably kicked more shins than balls, but he played soccer. He played well. So he was very, very popular. He had lots of friends. He got picked early for soccer matches, rather than the last child. I think he developed socially extremely well.

Eliya: Through all the work of building the school and raising a child with disabilities and running your business, how were you managing?

Jul: I think that we felt it was a job that had to be done. And you didn't really have time to be upset and worry. Of course, yes, we worried and worried whether we would cope financially with what had to be done, and eventually we worried for the whole school, not just about having a program for Avi. The school became an issue. A lot of work had to be done for the school.

But thank G-d, the school thrived. It consistently, year after year, won government awards as being one of the best schools in England, and that's even though we devoted thirty percent of the day to Jewish studies.

Years later we even got the Israel Prize from the State of Israel for what we had achieved for Jewish education outside of Israel. In fact, when we were awarded the prize, they phoned me up and said, "We have decided to award you the prize," and I said, "I'm really sorry, but it's not for me. It is for the school. I refuse to accept the prize personally. The head teacher, everybody—this is a tremendous work by everybody," and that's how it became.

At the award ceremony, the President of Israel *handed me the prize*. It should have been handed to my wife; she was the originator and mover in the school, not me. But it is still a man's world, I guess.

Eliya: What was it like for you, becoming a public figure?

Jul: That's an interesting one, because before the school we were never public figures. We used to have a joke in the family that Elaine's mother was the head of MI5, the English Secret Service, because they were so secretive about everything. In the house every cupboard was locked. When her mother and father used to go out somewhere, Elaine would ask, "Where are you going?" and they would say, "We're going to see somebody about a dog." Nothing was ever discussed.

And suddenly, yes, we were thrust into the limelight. It took time. We had to deal with it. I remember years later, my wife said, "You know, it's terrible. I can't go down the street without people recognizing me, and I'm not sure I like it. Everybody recognizes me." But that was the downside of it. But was it a downside? I don't know.

One true downside of the school being so good and so popular was that within a few years it, too, was oversubscribed, and we had to turn parents away. Parents whose children were admitted were personally grateful. We had a hard time resisting gifts from people who were grateful that they got their child into the school.

Parents whose child we didn't accept, on the other hand, became angry. To deal with being oversubscribed, we instituted a system whereby applicants who met the religious requirements for admission would go into a lottery. We would literally put names in a hat and we took the hat to the headmistress of the school up the road and asked her to draw the lot. Why? Because everybody in town would say to me, "How much does it cost to get my child into your school?" They wouldn't believe us that we had a system for selection. And they'd say, "But we know for a fact that it costs so-and-so much." And we said, "No. There is no price. It's a lottery, and Mrs. Dubs is the one who pulls the names out of the hat." So some people remained angry. Others were very grateful.

Eliya: You were a businessman and not a school administrator. How did you deal with the challenges of governing a school?

Jul: I would have to admit that my wife took the brunt of the responsibility, of the work, of the focus to actually get this solved. I would possibly have given up earlier, but there was no way she would give up. It had to be seen through, and thank G-d, we had such Heavenly help.

Eliya: At the Independent Jewish Day School you had the control to design programs which directly met Avi's needs. What happened when Avi graduated from IJDS and went to high school?

Jul: By the time Avi was ready to leave the Independent Jewish Day School, he was eleven, the age when our kids transfer to high school. The school of choice then was the Hasmonean Boys School, which was the only other Voluntary-Aided Jewish school. It still had only three classes for boys and three classes for girls. But also at that stage it was the law that you had to take disabilities children into mainstream education.

And Hasmonean complied one hundred percent. They took one of their teachers, who was in fact my old classmate, and put him in charge of the disabilities program. It was a big school, with four hundred boys. Hasmonean built a special wing to provide for the many different types of disabilities children they admitted. It wasn't just Avi. There were ten or fifteen children there.

Avi was placed in the regular class, but taken out for individual help. When he was out getting special help, it would happen sometimes that he would miss out on something introduced or explained by the regular classroom teacher, and we would have to find somebody to help him with what he missed. A new subject shouldn't have been taught while kids were withdrawn, but it couldn't always be avoided. The "pull-out" arrangement is not perfect, but I think on balance it was the only available solution.

One of the struggles we had in Hasmonean, and then later at IJDS, was to make sure that there was clear communication between the class teacher and the disabilities assistant. Even though we had special programs to teach the teachers how to work with the assistants and with the program, that communication struggle went on for years. Not just with Avi, but also with other children.

I think Avi did well in school. He did his matriculation. We had a lot of help at Hasmonean and Avi thrived in the school. My wife and I were not so much involved because Hasmonean had developed their own programs for disabilities.

Eliya: What plans did Avi make for after he graduated from high school?

Jul: Avi didn't apply to university. He said, "Let me go to yeshiva (advanced studies in Jewish text) and depending on how it goes I'll either apply to the university or not." He came to yeshiva here in Israel.

Eliya: How did you react to the idea of Avi leaving the protected environment of home and school, and going on his own to yeshiva in Israel?

Jul: What was it like for me having him away from home? That was an occasion where there was a shock. But it was easier for me than for my wife. I've always had the view that it's our job to give our children the tools to get on in life. But actually, it's *their* life. They're not our property, not our possession. We've got to enable them to fly the nest. I think my wife found that more difficult. She'd always been very close to her parents. She did everything for her parents, right up to their last days.

And I was different. I didn't live at home for many years. As a youngster, I went to boarding school, so I always felt that parents are great and important, but they don't own you, and I don't own my children. My responsibility is to enable them to get on with life by themselves.

Did I trust that Avi could take care of himself? Look, it's frightening sometimes. He phones now sometimes and you can hear that he's talking on the mobile phone in traffic, walking on the street. And my wife says to him, "Avi, don't walk on the street and talk on a mobile phone! It's too dangerous." And he says, "Okay, Mommy." But, thank G-d, so far he's had a guardian angel.

Eliya: How were you able to find a yeshiva for Avi that would accommodate his needs?

Jul: We had met a very, very nice young Englishman in London who was the spiritual counselor for a small yeshiva in Jerusalem, a real educator and a really warm person. He had come to recruit students in England. We knew his family, and he made a fantastic impression. We said, this is a smaller yeshiva, it's in Jerusalem. And my wife said, "I think I can entrust Avi to him." Avi had already picked this yeshiva for himself based on what other boys were saying about it. So it was easy for us all to agree.

What we didn't know was that just prior to Avi arriving in Israel, the yeshiva moved from a neighborhood close to the center of town to one much further out. What we discovered when we arrived there was a shock to us. They took us to a dormitory building where there was only one light bulb working. There were no handrails on the stairs. Avi could have fallen down those stairs at any moment. When my wife saw the staircase and the one light bulb she was terrified. Absolutely terrified. We were on the verge of saying, "This is no good."

But Avi said, "Just take me down the stairs once and I'll go after that by myself." And he insisted on staying there and he did extremely well. It turned out to be a great yeshiva for Avi. He had tremendous, tremendous Rabbis to teach him. Even after Avi left the yeshiva the Rabbis kept in touch with him. Several came years later to Avi's wedding.

Eliya: How did Avi fare without all the technological assistance he was accustomed to in high school?

Jul: He was able to read with the page right up to his nose. His glasses had enormous magnification. I don't think we managed to get stuff photocopied and enlarged. But he did have a closed-circuit TV there on which he read the sacred texts.

Best of all, he had teachers who really put a lot of energy into learning with him. Then one day, Avi announced, "I'm learning for rabbinic ordination!" I thought it was absolutely tremendous. It was a bit worrying for me if he would be able to hold his own. Since the students preparing for ordination get into some complicated legal arguments, I didn't know how Avi would be able to keep up. But Avi held his own. He has a tremendous memory and he learned the material and the sources extremely well. He could answer a challenge, saying, "What are you talking about?" And then cite the exact location in the text for his response. Eventually he got his ordination.

Eliya: Jul, you were thrust into a situation when your son was nine months old, and you just took it and kept moving with it.

Jul: We had no choice. And because we had to move with it, we had no time to be upset about it. Occasionally a thought creeps in... I remember once, years ago, we went to Belgium on holiday. There was a spot where you could actually take the car up to the beach, on the sand, and I said to Avi, "Avi, do you want to try and drive?" And he loved it. He drove the car—he couldn't do any damage to anything. You could see that he had such pleasure from it, but I felt, "What a shame." It was actually one of the worst moments for me. To see that he would never drive a car. And the joy he had from driving that car. There have been other moments like that.

There are many things he can't do. He knows it and I know it. And we have to cope with it. But when it affects his happiness, that's actually more upsetting to me than his limited mechanical ability, his technical ability.

Eliya: You made reference earlier to the fact that you couldn't spend time with your other boys as you would have liked. How did the brothers get along with each other?

Jul: I think they got on reasonably well. They had their tensions. They had their arguments, but they were usually arguments over substance, not over feelings or things like that.

Today, they're all good together. Number four, the baby, married the sister of Avi's wife. So they have double exposure to each other. But, yes, I think they get on well. Certainly, our grandchildren are great with each other, within each other's homes.

Eliya: You worked very closely with your wife to raise Avi and build the school. What was it like working together?

Jul: Fair question. The truth is, we've always worked together. Even in my feather-processing business, we'd worked together. When we were engaged, my wife used to come down to the factory and phone potential customers, saying, "Would you be interested in seeing quilts?"

And of course they would all say, "What are quilts? We use blankets in England." So we launched the product in England. We worked together then and we're still working together now.

Eliya: Looking back thirty-eight years, do you ever think about what might have been if you had not heeded the first doctor's advice to stay on antibiotics and instead sought another doctor's opinion?

Jul: Occasionally we have felt pangs of blaming ourselves. Should we not have accepted this doctor's instructions? We were newly married, still very naive about doctors. Today I've become extremely cynical about the medical profession, because I work in the medical field and I can see the rubbish that they sometimes produce and the way they work. But I'm convinced that families where the child is actually born with a problem, I reckon they blame themselves a lot more. "Is it something genetic that *we* caused? Is it our fault?" I don't know, but I suspect that the self-blame issue is much bigger when a child is born with a problem and that can, I think, to some extent also be paralyzing.

Eliya: What has been particularly rewarding about all the work you and your wife have done to make a school program to fit your son's disabilities?

Jul: Thank G-d, we've been able to help children in the school through our policy of mainstreaming. We've become great friends with parents because of it. But even more rewarding is when for instance, we see a girl with Down syndrome at the wedding of friends she made in our school over twenty years ago. She still is friends with those girls from school. We have seen this with the boys also.

Eliya: Most fathers of children with disabilities meet the challenges that are presented to them. But few take the challenge and use it to build schools or institutions. How did you do that?

Jul: Very simply, I have the greatest wife in the world, without whom none of this would have been possible.

Eliya: Thank you for talking with me, Jul.

12

AARON

_____

An integral part of Aaron's religious practice is to seek the advice of his Rabbi on all matters of both spiritual and personal concern. At the time of his daughter's birth, Aaron was in New York attending to his father who was critically ill. Aaron did not know that his newborn daughter had Down syndrome until he returned to Israel two weeks after her birth. Aaron's Rebbe (his spiritual teacher) advised his wife not to tell Aaron of their daughter's condition until he returned from caring for his father. (Note: Throughout the interview Aaron uses the Hebrew phrase "Baruch Hashem," which means "Praise and thanks to G-d.")

Eliya: Aaron, how old is your daughter and where is she in the family lineup?

Aaron: She was born about six months ago. She's the youngest of seven children.

Eliya: Did you have any indication during the pregnancy that she might have Down syndrome?

Aaron: No. We didn't do any tests. I mean, even if we had found out there was a problem, what practical difference would it have made? Would we have elected to "terminate," G-d forbid? Certainly not. G-d gives what He gives.

Eliya: Nobody said to you: "We see something and maybe we should find out more?"

Aaron: What was there to see? If there were any ultrasounds done for any reason, we explicitly told the technician not to tell us whether the baby was a boy or a girl. Anyway, ultrasounds are not so clear. As it happens, one of the ultrasound nurses asked us: "So! Who are you going to have come to do the ritual circumcision? Do you have a big family in America who will be coming for the celebration?" I don't know what that nurse saw exactly—we had a girl!

Before having our daughter, we did have a question as to whether or not we should continue to have children, because we are older parents. I am 51 and my wife is 45. My wife had read her share of warnings in the pregnancy books and she was in touch with health practitioners, from traditional doctors to alternative birthing counselors—and she certainly read everything available online.

So we heard all the scare stories and we were aware of the issues.

We asked our Rebbe: "Can we continue to have children?" And our Rebbe told us he sees no reason why we should not. In our twenty years of following the advice of our Rebbe, he has never been wrong. Not once. Letting our family grow naturally and accepting children when G-d sends them was the responsible, G-d-fearing thing to do.

Eliya: You were not able to be with your wife at the birth. Is that correct?

Aaron: Yes. I was in America visiting my father—he's since passed on, may he rest in peace. He was quite ill at the time.

My wife called me from Israel and she said, "I'm going into labor." She was two weeks early. And I said, almost like a joke, "Stop it. Don't do it. I'm not there." She said, "I'm going to the hospital. Bye!" And that's all I knew for many, many hours. I was waiting for a phone call, waiting to hear from someone—anyone. It was a long time before I got a call from my wife's birth coach. She said: "Congratulations—it's a girl!" And that's all I knew.

Eliya: What were your feelings when you heard that your wife gave birth?

Aaron: *Baruch Hashem!* It's a tremendous thing. And it was wonderful news for me and my aging Dad. It was the perfect kind of joy to raise his spirits. Well, I didn't know it, but back in Israel, there was an entirely different drama unfolding.

After the birth, my wife was allowed only a few minutes to hold the baby—that's unusual. Usually the midwives let the baby sleep on the mother's tummy. I would later find out from my wife that the midwives quickly gave the baby to the staff from the hospital nursery. And after asking, and then eventually pleading that someone should bring back the baby, my wife was told several times: "You've seen the baby already; the doctor hasn't yet."

This was very unusual. My wife was completely baffled by the hospital's responses to her. The next day she was called to the nursery. She said there were various people gathered around the crib. Some looked like nurses, others looked more like managers or doctors. They began asking her questions. "Madam, do you recognize this kind of child?" My wife had absolutely no idea what they were talking about. Then they told her the baby had Down syndrome, and they showed her all the signs—the shape of the fingers, the shape of the ears and the eyes. They said that they needed to do blood tests to confirm the signs, but they already recognized all the signs of Down syndrome. They told my wife that she just had to accept the baby's condition.

She was completely devastated. When she had some strength a few hours later, she called our Rebbe. And he told her, "Do not tell your husband about what the nurses are telling you." Just say, "*Baruch Hashem*, the Creator of the world sent us a new baby. Your husband's primary obligation now is to his aging father." My dear dad had cancer and was barely living. I needed to be completely focused on my dad. The Rebbe understood.

I happily told my dad, "Congratulations, Zaidie, you're a grandfather again!" He understood that much. But his memory was going, so every so often I would tell him again to give him joy—and each time I told him he was just as surprised and happy as the first time I told him!

Eliya: And the whole time you were in New York, your wife did not say anything to you?

Aaron: Absolutely not. Our Rebbe told her not to. On the phone she only said, "*Baruch Hashem*, we have a baby girl! And the doctors say she's doing fine. And my birth coach was with me during the birth, and I'm sorry you weren't here, but Hashem had me go into labor early." So it's all from Heaven. She really kept it all to herself. And she had no one to talk to. Can you imagine that? She spent those two weeks from the birth until I returned to Israel reading everything available online—and waiting for the results of the various blood tests that were done after the birth—hoping to hear that the delivery room nurses were mistaken.

Eliya: Tell me about your return home.

Aaron: About two weeks after the birth I flew back from New York.

I came back feeling happy knowing I had done the very best I could to help my dad even though his medical situation was unstable. Happy that we had spent some truly wonderful times together during my visit. And of course happy in anticipation of seeing our new little girl.

Now that I was back we could begin thinking about what to name her.

I had no idea what the name would be. To know the name you have to see the baby.

Here's something interesting for your book that people should know. My Rebbe told me that when it comes to naming their children, parents have Divine inspiration. The baby's soul has an identity, and as you hold the baby and get to know the baby, you gradually become more and more aware of the name. My wife and I have seen this with our other children. For our boys, we agreed not to discuss names at all until the night before the *bris* (ritual circumcision). For our girls we agreed not to discuss names until the night before the actual naming in the synagogue. Then, the night before giving the name, we each took a piece of paper and wrote down the top five or six names that seemed most appealing. Then we compared our lists— and with most every one of our kids, the first name on our lists matched each other. On the one hand we were astounded every time. On the other hand, our Rebbe told us it works, so it was no surprise.

So when I arrived from the airport, I was really excited. I walked in and found my wife nursing the baby. We talked for a while until she finished nursing—and during this time she still said nothing about our little girl's suspected condition. I was all smiles—but my wife was noticeably quiet, even somber. She tried to force a smile. I attributed this to general exhaustion. Thinking back, I think even my smiles were somewhat forced: in the back of my mind I knew my dad was dying. But I didn't want to make my wife sad, so I was going to wait several days before talking about my dad's condition.

My wife said to me, "Here's the little sweetie!" I picked her up and it was great. Newborns have this wonderful smell—fresh from heaven.

And I held our little girl and just kissed her forever. And she looked just like every one of our other kids when they were first born. After a while I said to my wife: "I have no clue what the name is—do you have a name yet? Don't tell me!"

About ten minutes later my wife said to me, "You should know... You should know that at the hospital they told me...some information. Something you should know about the baby."

She said, "They're doing more tests but they believe that she...uh...that she has Down syndrome." I looked at the baby and I said, "What? No. I don't think so.

And even if so—if that's Hashem's will, we'll take it. We'll handle it—okay."

Eliya: That was your reaction, "Okay"?

Aaron: On the spot. "If so, then okay."

Eliya: How do you account for being able to accept so easily the concept of having a child with disabilities?

Aaron: We have a Rebbe. He gives us guidance, and we do our best to take his direction. And with all of our questions throughout our years of marriage—major ones and even simple ones—we've asked our Rebbe and we've tried our best to follow his advice.

So when the Rebbe told us that it was okay to have another child, even though we were older parents, it removed any doubt or hesitancy we might have had. Whatever G-d would send—whatever G-d wanted of us—was clearly in the category of "okay."

Eliya: Did your wife also share the feeling that it was okay?

Aaron: There's no choice once you see how G-d is orchestrating a situation. "Okay" does not mean we retreated into robotic servitude, numb to the sobering situation and to the difficulties and to the disappointments that surround a Down syndrome birth. "Okay" means we understand there is a Higher Wisdom operating in every facet of worldly events and we must accept it and grow with it. I mean, the alternative would be to become grumpy, bitter and essentially angry at G-d—not a good setup for a person who wants to have a great Jewish future. It is true though that "okay" came easier for me than for my wife.

During the two weeks between the birth and my return to Israel, my wife spent most of the time in a rest facility for mothers who just gave birth. They give them lots of big meals and lots of time to rest and recover. It's great for them.

But she was in pieces, because she was by herself trying to handle this. At the rest facility my wife shared a room with a woman who had a child with disabilities whose condition was much worse. Severe—critical—not healthy at all. Every four hours there were nurses and doctors coming in to check that baby. That little soul was born into a world of tubes and wires. My wife learned to say early on: "We really have to say *Baruch Hashem*, even for a Down child. The way Hashem formed our little girl is the exact way He wants her to be.

So at that point, we understood that there's a spectrum. We realized that Hashem could have put us into a situation that was medically worse or would have been much harder for us to handle. But, He sent us what He knew we could handle and that is another reason why everything that happened was "Okay," and continues to be "Okay." It's simply our job—our work in this world, not to get in the way of Hashem's will.

So, I'm holding our little girl, and my wife says, "I read in an article there are people who have signs but turn out to be normal." I said, "So we're not going to lose hope." My wife had asked our Rebbe: "What are we to think with all the doctors saying that our girl has Down syndrome?" And the Rebbe said, "Things will be okay." If our Rebbe says it'll be okay, it'll be okay. And it is.

Eliya: You've described how you and your wife are completely accepting of your daughter having Down syndrome, but at the same time you sound very challenged by it.

Aaron: Look, the one thing they told us at the various meetings and conferences we've had at the hospital and with the social workers was that in spite of their limitations, Down children tend to be smiley and friendly and loving. Right now our baby is smiling and she gurgles and she's rolling over and doing wonderful things. And the physical therapists say, "Oh, she's doing so nicely!" But in years to come, when she stops being baby-cute and starts to get a personality, who knows what that personality is going to be? Will she be able to navigate normative society? Who knows if she will be made fun of in the street? Who knows what will happen? We think about all these things and the mind starts racing.

And we know that Down syndrome kids rarely get married. Yes, there are the special exceptions that get articles written about them, and it makes the pop-news for a couple of days. And it is wonderful. Of course we never hear whether or not the marriages last.

What about the vast majority of special kids who will never get married? They stay with their parents and they become fixtures in the home. We're assuming that, G-d willing, our little sweetie is going to be living with us for the rest of our years.

Eliya: Do you worry about these things?

Aaron: Worry? No. But there are infinite possibilities and Hashem has His plan. And we know lots of prayer is required. So one should say that clearly it's a wonderful thing to be the parents of such a child. But, we're human. We're people. And as parents, well, we weren't expecting to be challenged in faith and prayer under these circumstances.

Eliya: How have your other children reacted to their little sister?

Aaron: We haven't told them that there is anything different about her. All the kids get the same love and attention, and care and cuddling.

Eliya: What made you decide to keep that information from your children?

Aaron: Because we asked for advice from our local Rav (Rabbi), not our Rebbe, but the Rav in our neighborhood. He said, "Don't tell anybody who doesn't need to know. As a rule, we don't tell people difficult, painful news unnecessarily."

The Rav said, "If they don't ask, don't tell. Whatever they see on the child's face, so they see... Go about your life. Get busy with your life. Don't make it into a big thing."

Eliya: What outside resources are you using to help your daughter develop?

Aaron: We do what we can. She is receiving physical therapy and hydrotherapy and other types of learning therapy -- and our kids play with her and give hugs and kisses and love.

Eliya: Do you feel the need to seek support from any source?

Aaron: My support is from Hashem. There's prayer. I'm not going to any men's groups because I don't want to get pulled into other people's life dramas—we have enough drama already.

To get support we ask the Rebbe. We gain empirical wisdom by learning from our sacred texts. We get support from what we know, from past experience. At first, I did call a couple of friends to try to get support. But I soon realized that I had to find support from within me.

Eliya: What particularly challenges you about having a daughter with disabilities?

Aaron: I didn't want to be a parent to a disabilities child. This is the last thing on earth that I would ever have wanted for myself. I have always imagined how difficult it must be for someone to face the world without all his faculties. Thank G-d, when our baby is cute, she's like any other baby. When you play with her and she smiles and makes little noises at you, she's really cute. When she kind of spaces out, like Down kids can do, then her face changes and she looks like a Down kid. And that is frightening.

Let's stop the interview here. G-d has His way. It would be a big *chutzpah* (nerve) for me to say, "G-d! You sent the wrong person, the wrong baby!" Just like it would have been a big *chutzpah* to say when my father was dying, "G-d! You're taking the wrong man at the wrong time—I still need him to be a father to me." If you don't accept what Hashem sends, you can't live in His world.

Eliya: Thank you for letting me interview you, Aaron.

13

ELI

When Eli Shine heard that his son had Down syndrome he was in shock. But after literally a moment he let go of the shock and felt joy. When he was told that children with Down syndrome are characterized as happy and loving children, Eli believed that his son came into the world in order to spread happiness and love.

Eliya: Tell me about your son.

Eli: He was born exactly six months ago, to the day. He's the youngest of our five children. We had three girls before we came to Israel six years ago and since then we've had two boys.

Eliya: Did you have any indication prior to your son's birth that he would be born with Down syndrome?

Eli: No. Normal pregnancy. Everything was clear. All the ultrasounds were completely fine. The baby was kicking like crazy. Nothing at all pointed that way. This pregnancy was completely typical of the first four. And my wife is young as well.

She does say that she was way more sick in the beginning, but nothing to suggest a problem.

Eliya: When did you find out and how did you react?

Eli: From what I can remember in those moments before the birth I was completely helpless, especially since I was not certain what stage of the birth process my wife was at or what exactly was going on, so I was reciting Psalms. I didn't get very far because the actual birth was pretty quick. All of a sudden I heard, "Congratulations! Congratulations! It's a boy." I heard a very, very brief cry from the baby and then all quiet. I remember that the room was all quiet. My reaction when I heard, "It's a boy," was "Yay." It was beautiful. I was happy with that. I would have been happy with a girl also, but in some ways it balances the family a bit.

They brought the baby over to the baby warmer and they dumped him on it and left him there on his own, which I found a bit strange. I was standing kind of near to the baby warmer and they just plunked him down and ran away. No one talked. I could tell there was something weird going on. Why was everyone being quiet and not talking, and no one's staying with the baby? Something felt weird.

I looked at our son lying on the warmer and he was very, very placid and very purple. All our babies were purple when they come out, so I wasn't too worried about that. Something looked wrong, but I didn't know what. They brought in the pediatrician, who said something in Russian or Hebrew which I couldn't understand.

But I knew something was wrong and I looked at my son and wondered what it could be. What's the story? Is he okay? Is he not okay? Is he going to live? I looked at his face, and maybe it was the shape of his head or his eyes, but I said to myself, "I wonder if this is Down syndrome." I think I mentioned it to the pediatrician, and she said, "It looks like it, but we can't tell yet."

We had two birthing partners there with us. One was a close friend and one was her sister-in-law. And they came around and looked at me with a kind of look which said, "Yeah, it's true."

Our doctor's face was completely downcast, almost like he felt it was his own fault, like it was a bad thing.

Eliya: Where did you have the experience to know that perhaps these characteristics that you saw in your son's face suggested Down syndrome?

Eli: I've seen lots of kids around, so I've seen a certain look. I was familiar with it.

Eliya: What was your first interaction with your son like?

Eli: I guess at that point some negative thoughts went through my head. Worrying, and thinking, "What's it going to do for our family? How are we going to pay for it?" Or whatever else was going through my mind.

And then just seconds after that, I felt acceptance and said, "Can I hold him?" and they said, "Okay."

Eliya: What do you think helped you to so quickly feel acceptance?

Eli: One of the biggest helps was that I knew a couple of families in our community who had kids with Down syndrome, and they are beautiful examples of how families live with a special child. I thought: *Now we will be part of this exclusive club.*

I asked myself: *What's the good that can come from this?* I thought: *What better can there be for our family, for our kids?* Because ultimately the biggest struggle for kids nowadays is that they don't really learn how to give. There's no place for them to give. So this would be a good opportunity for them.

One thing that might have helped --I never thought about this before—was that I grew up with a kid in my class in elementary school who wasn't Down syndrome, but he was definitely a kid with disabilities.

Eliya: What kind of relationship did you have with that child?

Eli: I was like one of his friends. I wasn't his closest buddy. He wasn't the same as everyone else. He didn't continue on in high school with us, but we're still in touch. He's a nice guy.

Eliya: How did your wife react to hearing that her newborn had Down syndrome?

Eli: My wife didn't know that our son was Down syndrome. No one had told her. It was the first challenge presented to me by my new son: Who would tell her?

I tried to get the birthing partner to tell her. She was very experienced and I thought maybe she'd be able to do it. She said she couldn't do it. She and the doctor both said, "Take your son to the ward and we'll tell your wife in a couple of hours." I said, "No, no. There's no way you're going to take him away and not tell my wife." So I took him in my arms and I worked up the courage, took a deep breath and said to Abigail, "We have a special baby." And she said, "Ah! Such a special baby."

The first time I said it she didn't get it. So I said, "Just so you should know, this is a *special* baby. He has Down syndrome. We can't be sure, but it looks like it." And she was truthfully okay with it. Immediately. I didn't know whether she would be, of course. It's one thing for me to accept it. I knew I wasn't going to be the main player. I didn't have our son inside of me for nine months.

It was a beautiful fortune we had that my wife and I both felt acceptance. I used to say that I had thoughts of fear and thoughts of love, and I chose love. But since then I've come to think that love chose us. I don't think feeling love for our son was a choice. It just happened.

Initially, it was a shock for sure. It was definitely a shock. But there was no feeling down or upset or angry or "Why did this happen to me?" It just didn't really register.

Eliya: Did you have expectations before the birth of what would be for this child?

Eli: We all have expectations. We want our kids to be happy and healthy and independent and get married and all that kind of stuff. I don't know at what point it came to me, but I believe that there is a certain freedom in having a kid with Down syndrome, which is that you don't have to conform to everything that everyone has to conform to. Like if he didn't get married, people wouldn't be surprised and shocked and saddened.

In fact, if he did get married, people are more likely to raise their eyes, "Oh, wow! He got married"...that kind of thing. So that kind of eases the pressure.

Even the whole development thing. He's not expected to do this by this age and that by that age. They can't tell you, "He's likely to be really slow." Of course, they can't really know that. Because Down syndrome is really just a different statistic and there are kids who don't have Down syndrome who are very behind in their development and there are people with Down syndrome who are, in many areas of their development, actually above average.

I've actually heard of some people who go through life with Down syndrome and never have it diagnosed. They don't know that they have it. It's kind of an interesting twist.

What would have happened if he had never been diagnosed? We would have just taken him as a normal baby, and maybe he would need some extra therapy. It's interesting. I don't know how that would have been different. We'll never know.

I'm obsessed with personal development. Maybe being able to accept my son's condition came from my own work on myself. One of the things that I'm good at in my own life is being able to say, "Okay. So this is it. Now what?" I'm quite a pragmatic person.

The beautiful thing about Down syndrome is that it is what it is. Okay, you can work with it. But ultimately it's not going to change, it's not going to go away. You just have to work with it.

Eliya: Was your son's health at birth a challenge at all?

Eli: Yes. For the first few hours he was under observation in the main ward. The oxygen level in his blood was not stabilizing so they put him in an incubator. He was then moved into the infant intensive care unit. That first day he received oxygen, but did not need it after that. He was getting better, but, frustratingly, he wasn't improving completely. So it was a bit scary. He stayed in intensive care for two weeks. But in time his oxygen level stabilized, and now, generally, he's really healthy.

Eliya: During the time when your son was at risk did any of your attitudes change?

Eli: Before he had his cardiogram, I was definitely apprehensive and worried and thinking that I really hope that it's clear and good. But I didn't know.

Negative thoughts like "Why is this going on?" didn't come to me. The truth is, when you're in the incubator unit and looking at some of the other kids, there are different trajectories. The kids who make it through the incubator were small when they were born and they had all sorts of problems, but the problems can be dealt with and they become healthy and they can be fine. And that's beautiful.

On the other hand, our kid—who it turned out wasn't so severe in terms of his medical situation, but he's always going to have something. But it was much harder seeing other people who had been with their newborns in the hospital for months. It made me feel blessed, and also hearing that so many other kids with Down syndrome have serious heart problems and other things that really take their toll and we didn't, so I felt really grateful.

Eliya: How did your other children react when you told them about their new brother?

Eli: I decided I didn't want to tell my children on the phone so I only said to the children: "Congratulations! It's a boy." Our oldest daughter kept on asking me, "Is he healthy, is he healthy, is he healthy?" and I said yes. But I think she knew something was wrong. At that stage we were very careful whom we told that he had Down syndrome, because we didn't want the kids to find out from people before hearing it from us.

The truth is that the baby didn't look particularly Down syndrome at the time. In fact, there was even a doctor who said, "Ooh, maybe he's not Down syndrome."

But of course he was. So we could have gotten away without telling them, but that wasn't the point. We wanted them to know from day one. We wanted to be open with our children.

When I went home I sat the two oldest ones down, one at a time, and I told them, "This is the story." I said it in a positive way, and I was really happy about the birth and they could tell. I was completely open and authentic about it.

Eliya: What was their reaction to hearing that their brother has Down syndrome?

Eli: They'd seen handicapped kids before. They hadn't had much interaction with them, but they'd seen them. There was a little bit of apprehension. A few questions, a bit of wondering what their class would say. I assured them that we'll be behind them.

I said, "We'll speak to your schools, and don't worry." We did speak to the schools and the schools were great. They all came in and told the whole class that there are specially chosen families to look after children with disabilities. So it was an education for the whole class.

And of course, the whole class kind of rallied around my children as well, because having a classmate with a special brother was kind of an interesting thing. So that worked really well.

After we told our children, we decided that as soon as possible we would tell people outright. We wrote up a really nicely worded announcement and invitation to the pre-circumcision celebration [a celebration open to the community on the Sabbath night before the ritual circumcision]. It read: "With gratitude to G-d, we would like to invite all our dear friends and neighbors to a pre-circumcision celebration at our home this Friday night. We have been blessed with the privilege of bringing a special soul into the world who has Down syndrome, and we are grateful for this wonderful addition to our family. May we all have such joy from our children."

That was how we broke it to the world.

Eliya: How did the community respond to your announcement?

Eli: The pre-circumcision celebration was rocking. Unfortunately my wife missed it because she was in the hospital. There were hundreds and hundreds of people. People had never, never seen anything like it. It was really special. I think everyone felt something and felt our love and wanted to reciprocate and to give, and it was just amazing. We chose love and then we got it back a hundredfold.

We eventually got hundreds of emails from people, some from people we'd never met, who had children with Down syndrome. Everyone knows someone who's got Down syndrome, a relative or a friend. Word spread from the emails. Relatives and friends. Things spread.

Everyone wanted to help. The baby was in the intensive care and that was pretty difficult, but after that, he was just a baby and people wanted to help. And that was good because my wife was busy running to and from all kinds of therapies all the time. It took a lot of energy from her.

Eliya: Following the birth there is lots of attention paid to the mother. Did anyone give the father any special attention?

Eli: Within twelve hours of the birth two people turned up at the hospital. Each of them had a kid with Down syndrome. One was a man I knew from the neighborhood.

I was so happy to have someone there to give me a smile and a hug and let me talk. He said to me: "You can have lots of joy, and I'm sure he'll be a beautiful, happy, child." My friend was so positive and reassuring.

Eliya: Were you able to have the ritual circumcision ceremony as soon as you brought your son home from the hospital?

Eli: We had to wait a month, until his platelets went up, but the ceremony was very beautiful. Choosing the name was funny as well. We named him Tuvia Simcha. The name Tuvia somehow caught my eye and my ear about three months before he was born and I was kind of teasing Abigail about it. I would never have thought of choosing that name. It wasn't on our radar. But when it came down to it and he was born, it immediately became clear that that was the right name for him. *"Tuv Kah,"* the good of G-d. And certainly the idea of *tov* [good] is finding the good in situations. We thought that would be a nice mission for Tuvia, to see good and to bring out the good in people and in himself. And Simcha, which means "happiness" or "joy" seemed appropriate as so many kids with Down syndrome seem so happy.

Eliya: It's a very interesting idea that you frame Tuvia Simcha's condition as an indication of his life's work, that he can show the good, that his being in the world will help people to see the good in situations.

Eli: On the one hand, I feel like we're free from the expectations that we have of normal kids. He doesn't have to do everything specifically at every age that other kids do it.

At the same time, I'd love him to go very far. My wife has a favorite insight from the Torah: Why do we bless our children that they should be "...like Ephraim and Menashe" [A traditional blessing Jewish parents give to their children on the Sabbath]? Because Ephraim and Menashe went beyond their natural abilities. They were the grandchildren of the Biblical patriarch, Jacob, not his sons. All the other tribes were named for Jacob's sons, but they were upgraded when Jacob named them each an independent tribe. They achieved more than one would have expected given their natural abilities. That's the blessing that we give our children.

So we give it here as well. Part of me says, there's no reason why Tuvia Simcha can't do great things in the world.

We'd like him to be able to see his life as "I'm good; I can bring out the good in myself and other people," rather than "I'm less."

It's a reminder for us as well, to see the good in things. It's a nice way to live but it's not necessarily automatic.

We also realize that there are two parts to this: the original acceptance and then the following through with what you have to do. I guess in some ways we passed the test of him being born and the shock and the questions. That was something that somehow was natural for us. I don't know how. But it was and we are grateful for that.

But it's a test to work through with him over a lifespan, and please G-d, we should have the strength to do it.

Eliya: You said the pre-circumcision celebration was "rocking." What thoughts did you share with people there?

Eli: I spoke a few times, speaking from the heart. Speaking about how some people say, "Oh, I'm sorry" or stuff like that. Do you just say "Congratulations" or do you say the traditional blessing, "May he grow up to learn Torah, be married, and do all the positive commandments," or do you not say that? Maybe the child will not be capable of doing all those things. Or maybe having a child with disabilities isn't something to congratulate. I said that you can say that, that's fine. For certain you can say "Congratulations! May you have much joy," because children with Down syndrome give a lot of joy anyway.

I also said that people tend to say, "Congratulations! You should have the strength, all the strength you need to bring him up." It's funny, but I don't know why we don't bless parents of regular kids like that. They don't come and tell you, when you have regular kids, that there is about a twenty-five percent chance of delinquency, thirty percent chance of addiction or eating disorder, perhaps forty percent chance of deviating from the family patterns. But nobody says those kinds of things. But of course, these things happen and we have to deal with them.

All parents need strength.

Eliya: How did things change for Tuvia Simcha's siblings when he came home?

Eli: I don't think they changed so much. He was just a baby, like every other baby. His siblings adjusted to just having a baby. Maybe there was some extra attention required but I don't think it was too different from the past.

I think the beneficial effect of having Tuvia Simcha in the house will be more as he grows up. We will have to look after him and help him as he's growing. That's where I see the benefits coming for our children. Obviously there's the worry of whether we are we going to find the right balance of spending the amount of time with each child that he or she requires.

There are definitely challenges being the sibling of a kid with disabilities. But I think there are also real benefits and we've received a lot of encouragement. Some people who work in HASC [Hebrew Academy for Special Children in New York] tell me that the families who come to HASC are the happiest people in the world. It's kind of funny really.

Eliya: Has Tuvia Simcha needed any unique attention or therapies?

Eli: He needs some help with muscle tone and all that, so he's been having physiotherapy and occupational therapy. He's been having some speech therapy as well. Obviously he isn't talking yet, but we're strengthening the muscles around the mouth. We don't want to wait until he's behind to push him forward.

Eliya: Are you yourself involved in doing any of the therapies with him now?

Eli: No, I'm busy working now.

I'm inspired by my wife's efforts in doing all this. I'm not sure I would have the strength to do it all. We're giving him the best chance we can.

Eliya: So this brings us up to where we are now.

Eli: Yes, at the moment he's not that far off the normal developmental charts. Some doctors tell us he definitely will be. I don't know, could be. He might be, I don't know.

Eliya: I've heard a number of fathers say that they really think that their special child is "just for them," to help them in developing themselves.

You see, the funny thing about this, of course, is that kids with Down syndrome generally are happier than average kids.

Happiness and love are two of my biggest goals in life, to be happy and loving. So in some ways maybe Tuvia Simcha is in our family just for me. Having a happy and loving child, who can spread happiness and love in the world.

Yes. I'm excited to bring him up and see what he and I become.

Eliya: You both are going to do just fine, Eli. You should have much success.

THE LIFE LESSONS

It is not easy being the father of a child with disabilities. Every interview confirms this. Everyone faces challenges—that is what being alive is all about. However, the father of a child with disabilities faces more than most.

He must find solutions to a myriad of problems stemming from his child's medical, physical, cognitive, social, emotional, behavioral, and spiritual needs. He must deal with the stresses put on relationships with his wife, family, community, and professionals. He must educate himself in matters about which he may have little intrinsic interest. While coping with all these challenges he likely feels a range of negative emotions he may not know what do with, let alone acknowledge publicly. Add to all this the layers of stress all fathers have maintaining themselves and their families in today's uncertain environment. The fathers of children with disabilities who face their challenges and work to meet them are exceptional people with exceptional strengths and capabilities.

Each of the Chosen Fathers I interviewed reframed their challenges into opportunities for personal growth. They became better fathers, better husbands, and better human beings. Many of them will even say that while once their child was for them a source of pain, now it is a source of joy. How did they do it?

Chosen Fathers suggests four life lessons applicable to all fathers:

1. Build a team!

Our Chosen Fathers quickly realized: "I am not the only one challenged; so is my wife." They understood that having carried and nurtured this child, their wives may experience a whole range of feelings that they would never have. Wives typically have the physically taxing responsibility for daily care of their special child while maintaining other children, the house, and their husband. Each Chosen

Father made raising his child a team effort, giving his wife whatever physical and emotional support he could even if it meant putting aside his own needs.

Men are hard-wired to "go it alone" as the warrior, the explorer, the entrepreneur. To some men asking for help may be seen as a weakness. When it comes to raising a child with disabilities, asking for help is not only a strength, but a survival skill. When the demands on time, energy, and emotions become excessive (as they do), sharing the load is critical. When the negative feelings creep in (often lingering longer than one would like), having a teammate who understands those feelings and can offer comfort may save the day. When you don't know what to do next because you lack experience and knowledge about disabilities, having assistance to find the answers is a big relief. Difficult situations are more manageable when handled by a team.

When you feel incapable of dealing with never ending demands, you may become passive or even shut down. (Warriors, explorers, and entrepreneurs often have meltdown when they can't move forward.) Team building displaces passivity with action. As you expand the team to include family, community, and professionals you become a leader, a manager. The more the "team" operates the more confident you can be that a solution is attainable.

You can try to "go it alone," but the price to pay is astronomical. Most disabilities don't disappear over time; they continue to require a father's attention and energy for a lifetime. No family can afford to have a parent burn out.

A single parent may have no choice but to team-build. His survival and his child's depend on it. He must outsource whenever possible to family members, very good friends, and support agencies, or even consider hiring someone to share the load. All parents must guard their health and preserve their energy, especially the single parent.

2. Downsize your expectations, but have them!

Fathers naturally have high expectations for their children. We tend to see our children as an extension of ourselves. So their success becomes our success. It can be threatening to our self-esteem if we think our child is somehow imperfect or incapable of success. Think: how proud would you be if your child gets into the "best" school? Or makes the first string on the soccer team? It is natural to feel good about ourselves when our children succeed.

But what if we don't expect them to succeed, or expect only low level accomplishments? In their book *Don't Accept Me as I Am*, Professors Feuerstein, Rand, and Rynders answer:

> *Which is more damaging: to raise higher expectations and to struggle for their materialization, or to maintain low expectations and perpetuate nonadaptation and "happy" dependency? Not to struggle because of fear of failure leads to the passive acceptance of the condition as an immutable characteristic of the child. What is realistic for a child is determined to a great extent by our own goal settings, by the efforts we make in both planning and implementing interventions, by our continuous "dissatisfaction" with the stage of development already reached, by a persistent struggle to continue the process of growth and development.... (page 181)*

The professors assert that your child's achievement is directly related to the goals you set, your effort implementing the plans to reach the goals, and how much encouragement you give.

Honestly, I know you don't want to hear this. You don't need to feel burdened by another layer of responsibility and demand on your time and energy. But stop a moment, please, and realize that what the professors ask of you is no more than what you were prepared to give your child were he typical. Every one of your children needs you to have realistic expectations of him and her. Every child wants and needs his father to be his biggest fan; to root for him when the going is tough; to shout and cheer when he makes his goal; and to push him forward firmly but with love. A child develops confidence in himself when his father (and mother) demonstrates confidence in him.

After accepting your child and his condition unconditionally, having realistic expectations of him is a father's greatest challenge. We men are dreamers and builders. But if our dreams are crushed and we don't feel empowered to build our children the consequences may devastating to us. You may think: *If I don't expect anything then I won't be disappointed (or pained) if my child doesn't succeed.* Having no expectations is a safety mechanism which may provide relief, but only temporarily. Believe me, the next time you see your neighbor's child doing something typically age-appropriate and realize your child can't do it, the pain returns. So what can you do when you feel disappointed or you fear that your child will never succeed?

• First, know that what you feel is natural. You wanted a perfect child but that is not what you got. Each father interviewed for *Chosen Fathers* felt disappointment and sadness that his child was not what he expected and most likely never will be. Don't add to your negativity by getting down on yourself because you feel let down.

• Express your disappointment and sadness. Get it out. To your wife, a clergyman, a good friend, a therapist. Say: *I don't feel happy; I wanted something different for myself; for us; for my child.* The danger of keeping in your disappointment and sadness is that it can turn to anger. And anger is a powerful block to developing and maintaining positive relations with your child, your spouse, and yourself.

• Realize that having expectations is vital to your child's development, but they must be realistic. It isn't your child's limitations which are causing you problems. It is your unrealistic expectations that are the problem. No matter what limitations your child has he can grow and development from where he is into something more. If you expect it and encourage it.

• Successful educators (and parents) know to break "hard" tasks into small, doable steps. They never tell children that something is "hard to do."

If it is "hard" most children won't try; they won't risk failing their teachers, and certainly not their parents. Apply the concept of "Little steps for little feet" (coined by Dr. Ogden Lindsley to guide educators). In consultation with your child's therapists, teachers, and all the members of your team formulate realistic appropriate guidelines for your child's development. From the guidelines design the doable little steps for your child's little feet.

• Take pride in every accomplishment! The little steps may seem insignificant to you and they may be mountains for your child, but each step brings him closer to realizing his potential.

When my son was five and a half years old I thought he should learn to button his clothes. I did not want to be dressing him all his life. Given my son's hypotonicity (low muscle tone; also called floppy baby syndrome) his occupational therapist referred to him as a *shmatta*, a wet rag. She did not encourage us to spend the time training him to button. She said: *He can use zippers or Velcro.* For her it was easier but it wasn't better for my son. About the same time I read a book detailing "realistic" expectations of children with Down syndrome. Buttoning was not included in the list. (That was the last page I ever read in that book.) Maybe toddler clothing uses zippers and Velcro but adult clothing does not. So I insisted that we work on buttoning. We started with large three centimeter buttons and four centimeter vertical holes. It took close to three months of training before he pushed a button through the hole. His first do-it-himself button was a triumph that I still remember twenty years later. After six months he was able to button practically any button on any garment. Six months is a long time to spend learning to button a shirt, but consider how much independence those six months bought!

My son succeeded because we pinpointed buttoning as a goal; his team trained him in small, doable steps; and because we pushed for it. I became my son's advocate in learning to button. If you don't know this already, learn it now: no one will care more about your child than you (or his mother) do. No doctor, no therapist, no social worker, no friend, no relative! If you want your child to achieve his full potential then be his advocate. This is one opportunity for a major win/win: your child develops and you can take pride in his accomplishment and yours. This is a huge step for both of you.

3. It's your choice

A primary goal for all fathers is unconditional acceptance of their children. A father who is not at peace with his child will have great difficulty having peace with his wife, his family, his community, and himself.

From the interviews we learn that only one father (Eli Shine) "accepted" his son's diagnosis almost immediately. Most fathers must work through a range of negative emotions, doubts, and fears before they can truly accept their child's condition. Reaching unconditional acceptance is a process which may take a very long time and a lot of hard work. Sadly, some fathers never do the work.

"Shock" is the initial response of most fathers upon hearing that their child has disabilities. A limbo state often follows: one doesn't know exactly what he is feeling or what he is supposed to do next. He soon realizes that he has been robbed of joy. He may become angry. He may feel embarrassed or even guilty. The deluge of jargon from the professionals confuses him. The label "disabilities" conjures up a jumble of disconcerting images and associations. His thoughts darken and he is filled with negativity: *Why me? I can't handle this. I don't want this funny-looking kid.* He stands distant from his child, perhaps even blaming his child or others for all the upheaval in his life.

It's no wonder that there are fathers who want to abandon their child, leaving it for the hospital or "welfare" to provide a home. In the most extreme response, men have abandoned their child, and even their wives and family. Such fathers need deep professional psychological and/or spiritual counseling.

Most fathers, however, do not run away. But many withdraw. Withdrawal is a means of self-protection, an "out of sight, out of mind" maneuver. But when a father's heart is broken, withdrawal does not work for very long. At one extreme, fathers who withdraw have little or no interaction with their child and leave all the decision-making and care of the child to their wives. (My wife says that I was pretty much in "withdrawal" for the first three months after our son was born.) They retreat into their work or studies and keep their thoughts and feelings locked inside. They justify withdrawal by saying: *"My life must go on; it's up to me to keep everything afloat; I can't let anything interfere since I have to work even harder now, given the additional demands and responsibilities."* These fathers may also benefit from counseling, and they certainly need understanding, patience, and love.

In a more moderate stage of withdrawal fathers accept responsibility and share the care for their child with their wives. But they relate to their circumstances as a "burden to endure." Their emotional/mental state is still essentially negative. To successfully "endure" they push their thoughts and feelings deeper down. They remain distant from their child. They have no expectations for his development because unmet expectations will be another cause for disappointment and a reawakening of pain. Such a father does what he can to ease his wife's burden. He provides as best he can for his child's special requirements. He probably doesn't even complain. But he is not at peace. He doesn't love his child though he knows he should. He hurts and he is sad. But he works hard not to show it. What is he to do?

What did our Chosen Fathers do? Each, in his own way and in his own time, answered honestly a very tough question and then made a decision. He first let himself feel all his feelings: the sadness, the anger, disappointment, embarrassment, and guilt. And think all his thoughts: the burden, the deficiencies, the unattractive appearances, no hope for achievement, the expense, and the interruptions to his life. He stood back from it all and felt his "negativity." And then he asked himself: *Is this really how I want to be a father?* Feeling the full weight of his heart and mind, he answered: "No." He then made the choice to reframe his view so he saw something positive.

Every father has the choice of how he reacts to the circumstances of his life. But until he makes the decision to leave his darkness, he won't find the light. Each father must honestly face himself before he can find what works for him to start to love his child.

4. Believe that you were "chosen"

Several of the fathers interviewed state explicitly that they believe they were "chosen" to raise their child. I consider this belief to be the single most important factor allowing a father to release his negativity and approach his child in love.

I am a capable father

Being chosen implies that a father has within him everything needed to be his child's father. He may not have the technical knowledge or experience to know what stimulation and training his child needs. But how could he? There are literally hundreds of possible abnormalities that may disable a child which he likely never knew existed, let alone ever expected his child to have. And each child with one of those abnormalities has unique medical, psychological, social, academic, physical, and spiritual requirements. No father could know what his child needed. But he doesn't need professionals to tell him how to be a good father.

A man's innate sensitivities, his ability to learn whatever is required, and his desire to be an accepting, nurturing father is what every child needs. The professionals may know how to train a child's behavior, but they won't love and care for the child the way a father will. A chosen father knows that what his child needs most of him is just to be who he is, and always be there for him.

My son is not an "accident"

If you are chosen, then your child's condition is not an "accident." And if you are chosen then so is your child. His disabilities and your capabilities are a perfect match for each other. And if your child needs you to be his father, then you need him to be your child. This realization shouts out that there awaits you personal growth discoveries to be made from the way you relate to your child and how your child relates to you.

It comes out in the interviews that the fathers discovered strengths in themselves and truths about life that were a direct result of how they interacted with their child. The time frame for discovery differs from father to father, but when fathers got past their negativity the discovery process began.

I found new ways to connect with my son. I held him and talked to him and—though just an infant—I began showing him the world. I started to be myself with him. I began to act toward him as I had acted with my firstborn son. Even though I still did not know how my son would develop, I knew that I would do whatever was possible to encourage him. I began to learn about Down syndrome and how others relate to it. More and more I helped my wife to care for our son. Though my beginning with him was difficult I began to feel a deep love for my son that had been blocked. He was, after all, my son, and I am a father who loves his children. As I began to see my son as a gift I had received I was sure that I would eventually feel the joy that I was missing. Believing I was chosen got me started.

Whatever the "reason" I was chosen, it is for my good

When I heard from Professor Feuerstein that I was chosen (see Introduction), his words rapidly changed my mind-set, but my negative thoughts didn't magically disappear. It became obvious to me, however, that if I continued thinking negatively I would never approach my son with love. So I made a choice. I decided: *While I don't know at this moment why I was chosen, whatever the reason, from now on I will consider it is only for my good.* Making that decision changed my life. I began to see good where there had been none before.

My son's requirements and the demands on me didn't suddenly go away because I opened up to seeing "good." Nor did I suddenly "know" exactly what to do for my son. The extra financial expenditures continued. And my "team" didn't immediately recruit a second string to come in to relieve me when I was all played out. But all the heaviness that had been on me since my son's birth lifted when I decided that being "chosen" meant it was all for the good. I just had to be patient and let the good unfold.

I can't say there were never again dark moments. But when they crept in (which occurred many more times than I care to remember), I was resolute in my decision to find the good. If I wasn't immediately successful on my own, I sought help from my primary team mate, my wife.

Over the years my need to find "the" reason why I was chosen has disappeared. In its place I take pleasure in being able to "be who I am" with my son. It's okay to be silly with him. I can win or lose to him in checkers and either way we both come out winners every time. I can explain how things work in nature, with people, in life, because he wants to learn from me. We sing together, we arm wrestle. I am just his father and he is my son.

The concern and care for children with disabilities doesn't diminish when they become adults. Even though he now lives in an apartment with roommates, works as a landscaper, and wants to be married, my son will always be dependent on me. I must plan for his well-being at the time I cannot actively care for him. I don't have to do that for my two typical children; they will care for themselves. The road I and fathers like me walk is a very long one.

It is up to every one of us to decide what kind of father we want to be. If we decide to do everything possible to accept and love our children, we will. If we choose to distance ourselves from our children, our wives, and ourselves, we'll remain distant. If we want to grow personally from the unique experiences our children present to us, we'll grow.

A father just has to decide who he wants to be to his child and to himself.

And to know that any father can be a Chosen Father. If he chooses to be one.

THIS IS YOUR LIFE.
ACCEPT IT.
MAKE IT GOOD.

If you are a father of a child with disabilities and you have read *Chosen Fathers*, I salute you. You are not a father who is hiding from reality. Whatever emotional and spiritual state you are in right now you are open to find out how others are coping. (You picked up *Chosen Fathers*, didn't you?) This means to me that you may be looking for a way out of the head and heart space you are in.

If you just became a member of the club you feel confused and dark. The shock is great. You may feel ashamed of fathering an "imperfect" child. Despair commonly follows. You will need time to heal. How quickly and completely you heal, however, depends on you.

If you have been one of us for some time, your child is likely developing at some pace, and your systems are operating with some efficiency. You are no doubt calmer, better organized, but you wouldn't say you are happy or optimistic. Maybe what describes you is being in "neutral," the motor is running, but you aren't going anywhere.

If you are a father who unconditionally accepts his child, his situation, and finds joy in his life, bravo to you. Your head/heart space is where we all should be. You infuse the world around you with hope and energy. The programs and systems to support you and your child's needs are in place. You have worked hard to create a life that gives you satisfaction. I wish you would contact me to share your journey so together we can let other fathers know what awaits them.

If you are the mother of a child with disabilities (and the wife or partner of the father) much of what follows is also for you. You may be in touch with your true feelings and can articulate them clearly. But you are no doubt challenged by the physical and emotional upheaval that accompanies caring for your child. Helping the father to face his situation and accept it unconditionally may go a long way to relieving much of the burden that you feel.

The negativity that most all "just became" fathers fall into is not a good space. It leads to despair. It blocks effective decision making. If left unchecked it can destroy a marriage and scar children. I was in it for over three months after my son was born. My wife was not happy with me because I had pretty much "checked out." I am thankful that I met Professor Reuven Feurerstein who led me to reframe my perceptions. I heard from him that I "got a good one". All it took was a moment to realize how much I missed feeling positive. I decided then that I would find the good in my son.

I stopped comparing my son to a typical child and seeing only his deficiencies. I reframed my perceptions to compare my child to himself. I stopped looking at the age markers on the development milestone charts. Instead, I said to myself (and others): if I got a good one, then he will do good things; whenever he does them. I developed realistic expectations for his development. I learned to take pride in every step, no matter how small. Once I stopped lamenting my situation I began to build the systems I needed to help develop my son's strengths. And, gradually in the process, to discover and experience the joy of being his father.

Nobody asked you if you wanted to be the father of your child. It was thrust upon you unexpectedly. And with this unwanted circumstance come emotional, physical, financial, and social demands which don't stop coming. Only one father (Eli Shine) of the many whom I interviewed accepted unconditionally his son's disabilities within moments of learning about them. (But Eli, too, reveals that his initial reaction was shock and fear.) So feeling confused and despairing, and even feeling "neutral" are reactions that most all men have.

But the decision you must make is: I acknowledge my negativity and neutrality. Will I remain in this space, or will I decide to accept what is and find the good in it?

I am going to say it, though you may not like hearing it: you really have no choice. Your physical and emotional well-being depends on it. And likewise for your wife and family. Your attitudes and enthusiasm will energize all those around you.

So get busy and make life good.

Once you have decided to go for the good, start the reframe process by answering the following questions:

- What are you going to make of the life you now have?
- Are you in touch with your deepest feelings and can you share them honestly, or have you closed yourself off?
- Are you a full partner in raising your child, or do you avoid responsibility?
- What would make you feel joyous about being a father?

There are two books that may give you additional direction to reframe. *Not What I Expected*, by Rita Eichenstein, PhD, is a skilled clinician's description of how parents react emotionally when they learn that their child has a disability. Dr. Eichenstein identifies five stages of acceptance parents go through. *Not What I Expected* is a valuable tool for acknowledging "this is your life" and then "accepting it." (Find *Not What I Expected* at www.drritaeichenstein.com.)

Yvonne Newbold's three children have diagnosed disabilities and for most of her child rearing years she was a single parent. (We don't hear about what happened to that father.) She wrote *The Special Parent's Handbook*. (www.yvonnenewbold. com) which is the most honest and frank call to parents to "get busy and make life good" that I have ever read.

To decide to find joy in your situation and to then to reframe it, you must start somewhere. Talk out your situation. Turn to someone who cares about you, will listen to you, and will validate your feelings without judging you. Turn to a trusted family member or friend. (Perhaps your wife, but most likely she, too, is trying to accept her life and may not be able to give to you completely right now. In time, she can become your most trusted and helpful team mate. And you hers.) Maybe you have a compassionate clergyman. Or you can find a skilled coach. Your best arrangement, of course, is talking with another father who has been where you are. He will understand you quickly, completely, and will not judge you. You will be able to be yourself with him.

I am one of those guys. I will listen and show you how to reframe your perceptions. You may contact me and we can talk. Go to www.fathersconnect.com

and sign in, requesting to talk to with me. It will not cost you anything for that conversation. Or email me at eliya@fathersconnect.com. I will return your call.

While you are at the site:

- Learn how cost effective it is to reframe your negativity into joy
- Discover how Building 5 Teams will give you time to chill, sharpen the saw, spend private time with your mate, spend quality time with your other children, all the while developing your child to his fullest potential
- Download free and valuable resources that fathers need
- Read more of what I have written about being the father you are meant to be
- Find tips for the mother of your child which will help her to better understand and more appreciate you

But, please, above all, decide to make life good for yourself.

So you can become the father you are meant to be.

Please, if you will, let me know at my website www.fathersconnect.com or by email eliya@fathersconnect.com how you are doing.

Take very good care,

Eliya Stromberg

Made in the USA
Coppell, TX
02 November 2020